CW00631936

LITURGIES FOR

LENT

LITURGIES FOR WEEKDAYS

LENT

Flor McCarthy SDB

Reflections on Saints' Days

Vincent Ryan OSB

DOMINICAN PUBLICAITONS

First published (2007) by
Dominican Publications
42 Parnell Square
Dublin 1

ISBN 1-905604-02-5
978-1-905604-02-9

British Library Cataloguing in Publications Data.
A catalogue record for this book is available
from the British Library.

Copyright © (2007) The Authors and Dominican Publications

All rights reserved.
No part of this publication may be reproduced, stored in
a retrieval system or transmitted by any means,
electronic or mechanical, including photocopying,
without permission in writing from the publisher.

Cover design by David Cooke

Printed in Ireland by
The Leinster Leader Ltd
Naas, Co. Kildare.

Contents

Weekday Liturgies

Flor McCarthy

Lent and Its Readings

Lent began historically as a time of intense preparation of candidates to be initiated into the Church community at Easter. The Easter Vigil owes its origins to the practice of early Christian communities staying up all night to pray with these candidates. This was a time when the majority of those being initiated were adults.

But this season did not belong to the candidates for initiation alone. It also invited the rest of the community to join the candidates in prayer and penance. This was not only a means of support for the candidates, but also a time for the faithful to renew their original commitment to live out the meaning of their own baptism.

Eastertide began a fifty-day 'honeymoon' period for those who had been initiated into the Church at the Easter Vigil. During this time the whole community celebrated the new life these new Christians had given to the family of Christ, while the neophytes themselves learned to settle into their new way of living.

This baptismal focus was lost over the centuries when there were no more adults for initiation into established church communities.

However, the liturgy has been renewed in such a way that the baptismal aspect can be perceived more clearly. Hence, those important passages from the Gospel, which were read to catechumens in the early centuries to prepare them for baptism, are proclaimed.

These readings are directed to all the faithful, because during Lent the whole Church, along with those about to be baptised, calls to mind the mystery of its initiation into Christ.

SUNDAY READINGS

Here we are concerned only with the weekday readings. But since these are meant to complement the Sundays readings, we need to remind ourselves what the latter are about.

The Gospel readings are arranged as follows: The first and

second Sundays retain the accounts (from all three Synoptics) of the Lord's temptations and transfiguration. Thereafter, the Gospel of John takes over as the dominant source. The Church turns to John for insight into the profound meaning of the mystery of the Lord's death and resurrection.

On the third, fourth and fifth Sundays, the Gospel readings for Year A are the three great baptismal texts of the Samaritan woman, the man born blind, and the raising of Lazarus. Because these Gospels are of major importance in regard to Christian initiation, they may also be read in Year B and Year C, especially in places where there are catechumens.

Other texts, however, are provided for Year B and Year C: for Year B, a text from John about Christ's coming glorification through his cross and resurrection, and for Year C, a text from Luke about conversion.

On Passion (Palm) Sunday the texts for the procession are selections from the Synoptic Gospels concerning the Lord's triumphal entrance into Jerusalem. The Gospel for the Mass is from the synoptics account of the Lord's passion.

The Old Testament readings are about the history of salvation, which is one of the themes proper to the catechesis of Lent. The series of texts for each Year presents the main elements of salvation history from its beginning until the promise of the New Covenant.

The readings from the letters of the apostles have been selected to fit the Gospel and Old Testament readings, and, to the extent possible, to provide a connection between them.

WEEKDAY READINGS

The weekday readings work out, from day to day, the baptismal and penitential characteristics of the entire period. The readings (from the Gospels and the Old Testament) are placed in harmony with each other, so that different themes can be more fully expressed.

They treat various themes of the Lenten catechesis that are

suited to the spiritual significance of this season. However, from the Monday of the fourth week onwards, the Gospel of John is read in a semi-continuous fashion, to reinforce the baptismal catechesis of the Sundays.

In the first half of Holy Week the readings are about the mystery of Christ's passion. For the chrism Mass the readings bring out both Christ's messianic mission and its continuation in the Church by means of the sacraments.

———————————

Lent is a time of penance and effort. But it is also a season of joy because we are preparing for Easter. The daily readings of Lent present an abundance of riches. I have tried to tap into those riches, not just in the homilies, but in other parts of the Mass as well. In order to help to put the readings into their context, I have provided a Scripture Note each day. A lot of work went into the preparation of these brief notes. For me, they constitute the most important part of each day's fare.

Flor McCarthy

Weekdays of Lent

ASH WEDNESDAY

INTRODUCTION AND CONFITEOR

Lent began as a time of intense preparation of candidates who were to be baptised at Easter. But this season was also a time for the faithful to renew their original baptismal commitment.

Let us turn to the Lord and ask him to show us what we need to do in order to deepen our commitment to him during this holy season. [Pause]

Lord Jesus, through this holy season you give us strength to purify our hearts and control our desires. Lord, have mercy.

You give us a spirit of loving reverence for you, and of willing service of our neighbour. Christ, have mercy.

You teach us how to live in this passing world with our heart set on the world that will never end. Lord, have mercy.

SCRIPTURE NOTE

Judah was being laid waste by a plague of locusts. The prophet Joel (*First Reading*, Joel 2:12-18) uses this natural calamity as an opportunity for urging the people to come back to God. He calls for more than an external or cultic return to God; their whole conduct must change: 'Rend your hearts, not your garments'. They are to express their repentance by fasting. If they do, then God will have pity on them, because he is 'all tenderness and compassion'. Besides, he owes it to himself to deliver his people and his heritage. Lent addresses a similar call to us.

Paul reminds the Corinthians (*Second Reading*, 2 Cor 5:20–6:2) of the grace they have received when they accepted the Gospel. But he tells them that they will have received this in vain if they fall back into pagan ways. He urges them to make use of the present opportunity that is being given them. The same appeal is addressed to us. Lent is a favourable time to heed it.

Jesus (*Gospel*, Mt 6:1-6, 16-18) tells his disciples to beware lest they practise their piety in the wrong way and for the wrong motive. Good deeds must not be done for outward show but from a sincere desire to please God. He applies this principle to almsgiving, prayer, and fasting, three things that are traditionally associated with Lent.

REFLECTION — *An opportune time*

Nature shows us that there is such a time as an opportune time. For instance, there is a time for planting and a time for reaping. This applies to our lives too. We too have our seasons because we are involved in a process of growth.

From a spiritual point of view, Lent is an opportune time for us. There is something about Lent that spurs us into action in the battle against evil. Maybe it is the picture of the sinless Jesus battling with Satan in the desert. Lent calls us to prayer, penance, and works of charity. In short, to a fuller living of the Christian life.

In the Second Reading, St Paul reminds the Corinthians of the grace they have received when they accepted the Gospel. But he tells them that they will have received this in vain if they fall back into pagan ways. He urges them to make use of the present opportunity that is being given them. He says, 'Now is the favourable time; this is the day of salvation.' The Church applies these words to Lent.

Even though prayer, penance, and almsgiving are always appropriate, they are especially appropriate during Lent. There is such a thing as 'a window of opportunity', a moment of grace. Lent is a window of opportunity, and a season of grace.

Lent is the Church's 'holy spring'. During it the catechumens were prepared for baptism, that is, for their rebirth in Christ. And during it the faithful strove to renew their original baptismal commitment. It is a time of penance and effort. But it was also a time of joy. It is like springtime. As we progress towards Easter the sun gets brighter and warmer. So, as we journey through Lent, our hope grows, our joy increases.

ASH
2011

REFLECTION — *Come back to me with all your heart*

Through the prophet Joel God addressed his people with the words: 'Come back to me with all your heart.' It was a call to repentance, a call which is now addressed to us. The words of the psalmist are also addressed to us: 'O that today you would listen to his voice! Harden not your hearts.' This too is a call to repentance.

Lent is an opportune time to answer this call. St Paul might have been talking of Lent when he said: 'Now is the favourable time; this is the day of salvation.'

Lent calls us to a change of life, that is, to repentance. Those other words of Joel are very relevant here: 'Rend your hearts, not your garments.' He is telling us that repentance must not be something merely external; it must also be internal. It must involve a change of heart. Otherwise it will be superficial.

Jesus makes the same point in the Gospel. He says that good deeds must not be done for outward show but from a sincere desire to please God.

Lent is a time for conversion. The most important conversion of all is a conversion of heart. Each of us stands in daily need of a conversion from a closed heart to an open heart, from a heart of stone to a heart of flesh.

God is continually calling us into communion with himself. His call is essentially an appeal to our hearts. God longs for our hearts. In the words of St Teresa of Lisieux: 'If God hasn't got our hearts, he has nothing.' And we recall what Jesus said of the Pharisees: 'This people honours me with their lips, but their hearts are far from me.'

It is the heart that matters. A person is what the heart is. Our chief concern then must be to get the heart right. But only God can make it what it is supposed to be. Softened by the rain of his grace, and warmed by the sun of his love, the human heart can be turned from a desert into a garden.

Ash ✓
2011

REFLECTION — *Giving in secret*

A man (Andrew) tells how his workmate's wife developed cancer. It was a very worrying time for them because they had several children. An operation could cure her, but the doctor wouldn't operate on her because they didn't have the money. They asked Andrew if there was anything he could do for them.

The problem was that Andrew was broke. To compound matters, he was still on crutches after an operation. Nevertheless, he hobbled around the neighbourhood telling everyone the story.

He began to gather up the money. Fifty cents here, fifty cents there – money was scare back then. He managed to get about half of what was needed. He took the money to the hospital, but they said it wasn't enough. After a big fight, they finally agreed to perform the operation. The operation was a success. The woman lived and was able to raise her children.

Andrew says, 'Afterwards I had the greatest feeling. I felt the presence of God. It seemed to wrap me in a blanket. But then I told one of my best friends about it. And the minute I told him, that wonderful feeling left me. Then I got all this applause from all over the place. And it just made me sick.'

He concludes: 'If you do something for the applause of people, and if that's what you want, okay. But if you want to have the most wonderful feeling that comes from having God with you, keep it to yourself.'

The great paradox is this: those who look for a reward, and who reckon that it is due to them, do not receive it; those whose only motive is love, and who never think that they have deserved any reward, do, in fact, receive it.

Jesus urges us to do our good works in secret. God's loving eye will see our good works, and rewarded them in secret. The quiet reward is sweeter. True virtue doesn't draw attention to itself.

PRAYER OF THE FAITHFUL

Celebrant: At this favourable time, on this day of salvation, let us bring our petitions to God who is all tenderness and compassion.

Response: Lord, graciously hear us.

Reader(s): For Christians: that the observance of Lent may make them better disciples of Jesus. [Pause] Lord, hear us.

For those for whom fasting is a permanent condition due to lack of food. [Pause] Lord, hear us.

For those who are blind to their sins, and who see no need to change their lives. [Pause] Lord, hear us.

For grace to show our repentance by a new way of living. [Pause] Lord, hear us.

For our own special needs. [Longer pause] Lord, hear us.

Celebrant: God of love, hear our prayers. Help us to know your will and to do it with courage and faith. We make this prayer through Christ our Lord.

PRAYER/REFLECTION

Lent calls us to repentance.
But if repentance doesn't involve a change of heart,
it will not lead to a change of life.
It will be like decapitating weeds
while leaving their roots intact.
Lord, help us to turn our hearts away from evil,
and to set them firmly on pleasing you.

THURSDAY AFTER ASH WEDNESDAY

INTRODUCTION AND CONFITEOR

In his love for us, God is continually us to a deeper and more authentic life. Lent is a favourable time to respond to God's call. Part of what we have to do is to put right anything that is wrong in our lives. Let us reflect for a moment on what we need to change in our lives. [Pause]

Lord Jesus, you are all tenderness and compassion. Lord, have mercy.

You are slow to anger and rich in mercy. Christ, have mercy.

You turn your face from our sins but not from us. Lord, have mercy.

SCRIPTURE NOTE

The Israelites (*First Reading*, Deut 30:15-20) had a special relationship with God. But if they gave their hearts to false gods, it would spell the end of that special relationship. Hence, when they were about to enter the promised land Moses set a choice before them: to worship the true God or false gods.

If they chose to worship the true God, and to obey his commandments, their stay in the land would be a long and happy one. But if they choose to worship false gods, their stay in the land would be a short and unhappy one.

It was a choice between life and death, between a blessing and a curse. This stark choice was not meant as a threat. What comes across is Moses' concern for his people. He dearly wanted them to have a long and peaceful life in their new homeland.

After Peter had professed that Jesus was the Messiah (v. 20), Jesus told his disciples that the Messiah was destined to suffer, and that they too would suffer (*Gospel*, Lk 9:22-25). He confronted them with a choice: if they wanted to be his disciples, they would have to deny themselves and take up their cross and follow him. He promised life to those who chose to follow him.

REFLECTION — *The blessings of obeying God's commandments*

As the Israelites were about to enter the promised land Moses set a choice before them: to worship the true God or to worship false gods. If they chose to worship the true God, and to obey his commandments, they would bring a blessing on themselves. If they choose to worship false gods, they would bring a curse on themselves.

This was not meant as a threat. What comes across is Moses' concern for his people. He dearly wanted them to have a long and peaceful life in their new homeland.

We are faced with the same choice: to obey God's commandments or to disobey them. The commandments were made, not for God, but for us. To live according to the commandments is the best and wisest way to live.

Take a musical instrument. You can play it any old way, but if you do, it will sound awful and you will ruin it. But if you play it properly, it will sound good. To play it properly means to play it according to the rules of music, rules which are there, not to make music difficult, but to make it possible.

So it is with us. There is a right way and a wrong way to live. The right way is the way God intended. For this purpose he gave us the commandments. When we live by those commandments, we are living and functioning as we were meant to. We are like a musical instrument which is being played well.

The commandments are a sign of God's love for us. They teach us how to live. God wants us to have life here and hereafter, which is the real promised land towards which we are journeying in faith.

REFLECTION — *Choose life, not death*

Sometimes people need to be faced with a stark choice. Alcoholics, for example, need to be confronted with the choice: either you go on drinking and face an early and wretched death, or you give up drinking and have a long and happy life. This is not meant as a threat. It is done out of concern for them.

When the Israelites were about to enter the promised land, Moses set a stark choice before them: to worship the true God or to worship false gods. If they chose to worship the true God, they would bring a blessing on themselves. But if they choose to worship false gods, they would bring a curse on themselves. Moses was not threatening the people. What comes across is his concern for his people. He dearly wanted them to have a long and happy life in their new homeland.

However, there is a stubborn streak in us that causes us to go our own way against all advice. Without self-discipline freedom can be a curse rather than a blessing. To be free is to have choices, but choices have consequences. That's the basic point being made in the first reading.

The blessings that flow from obeying God's law are brought out in the responsorial psalm. It uses the beautiful image of a fruit tree that is planted beside a stream. Such a tree 'yields its fruit in due season and its leaves never fade'. That is the kind of full and fruitful life that is promised to those who follow the way of the Lord.

In the same way, when Jesus says that we must take up our cross and follow him, he is not laying a burden on us. He is calling us to life. It is a choice for life, even though it will inevitably involve a dying to self. True happiness is to be found, not in self-indulgence but in self-forgetfulness.

REFLECTION — *Pruning time*

Jesus says, 'If anyone wants to be a follower of mine, let him renounce himself and take up his cross every day and follow me.' He is facing us with a choice: to live for self, or to deny self and follow him.

When we live for ourselves, we are not living fully or happily. Selfishness leads to slavery – slavery to one's appetites and compulsions. On the other hand, to deny self is to be happy and fully alive.

However, to deny self is never easy. Words such as asceticism, renunciation, self-sacrifice, and penitence are not much in vogue today. But we must try to understand what they mean. They mean what pruning means.

Pruning time is a painful time for a fruit tree. The pruner rids it of all those suckers which use up a lot of energy but produce no fruit. However, the aim of this surgery is not to inflict pain, but to help the tree produce more and better fruit. Without pruning you get an abundance of leaves but little fruit.

Lent is a kind of spiritual pruning time. There is much that is useless and perhaps harmful in our lives, which saps our energy, and diminishes our spiritual fruitfulness. Of what shall we prune ourselves this Lent so that we may become more fruitful branches of Christ, the true Vine?

Jesus didn't ask of us anything he didn't ask of himself. He chose the way of suffering. It wasn't that he was in love with suffering. It was because he chose the way of love. And love inevitably results in suffering.

PRAYER OF THE FAITHFUL

Celebrant: Let us pray that we may know the blessedness of those who walk in the ways of the Lord.

Response: Lord, hear our prayer.

Reader(s): For the leaders of the Church: that they may give an example of true discipleship by lives of service. [Pause] Let us pray to the Lord.

For government leaders: that they may seek the wisdom that comes from God and his Law. [Pause] Let us pray to the Lord.

For those who are living selfish and irresponsible lives, thus bringing misery on themselves and others. [Pause] Let us pray to the Lord.

For all gathered here: that we may enjoy the freedom of the children of God. [Pause] Let us pray to the Lord.

For the strength to shoulder the crosses that come to us each day in the line of our duties and responsibilities. [Pause] Let us pray to the Lord.

For our own special needs. [Longer pause] Let us pray to the Lord.

Celebrant: Lord, accept our humble admission of guilt, and when our conscience weighs us down, let your unfailing mercy raise us up. We make this prayer through Christ our Lord.

PRAYER / REFLECTION

Lent is a kind of spiritual pruning time.
In pruning a tree,
the aim is not to inflict damage on the tree,
but to help it to produce more and better fruit.
Lord, show us what we need to prune ourselves of this Lent,
so that we may become more fruitful branches of you,
the true Vine.

FRIDAY AFTER ASH WEDNESDAY

INTRODUCTION AND CONFITEOR

Fasting is something that has always been associated with Lent.
When we hear the word 'fast' we tend to think of fasting from
food. That is one kind of fasting. But there is another kind –
fasting from wrong-doing. Without the second, the first is worth-
less in the eyes of God. [Pause]

Lord Jesus, you blot out our sins. Lord, have mercy.
You give us the joy of your help. Christ, have mercy.
You put a steadfast spirit within us. Lord, have mercy.

SCRIPTURE NOTE

Fasting is the common theme in today's readings. In the *First
Reading* (Is 58:1-9) Isaiah talks firstly about the wrong kind of
fasting. Fasting that is accompanied by oppression of workers
and exploitation of the poor is an abomination. God is not impressed by a religious practice that is divorced from a concern
for social justice. The prophet goes on to talk about the right
kind of fasting. Genuine fasting is necessarily linked with the
practice of justice and concern for the poor and the needy.

In the Old Testament marriage is often used to describe the
relationship between God and his people. In Jesus a new 'wedding' takes place (*Gospel*, Mt 9:14-15). He restores the broken
relationship between God and his people. This is a cause, not

for fasting, but for rejoicing. Jesus' disciples are like guests at a wedding. They do not fast because he is with them. They will fast when the bridegroom (Jesus) is taken away from them – a thinly veiled reference to his impending death.

For us any time is a good time to fast, but Lent is a particularly opportune time.

REFLECTION — *The fasting that is pleasing to God*

Fasting has always been associated with Lent. However, when we hear the word 'fast' we automatically think of fasting from food. But there is another kind of fasting – fasting from wrongdoing.

At the time Isaiah was writing, fasting in the ordinary sense was taken seriously by God's people. Fasting is meant to be an outward sign of something that is happening inside a person. Unfortunately their fasting was just an outward show of religiosity. In reality their hearts were turned away from God.

Even so, they complained that God took no notice of their fasting. Isaiah told them why God took no notice of their fasting. It was because even as they fasted, they went on doing business on holy days, oppressing their workers, quarrelling and squabbling with one another, and exploiting the poor. That kind of fasting was totally ineffective from a spiritual point of view.

Then he went on to tell them the kind of fasting that was pleasing to God. He told them to fast from any form of wrongdoing against their neighbour. For instance, they should stop exploiting their workers and oppressing the poor.

True repentance involves ceasing to do evil. But it also involves doing good – living what is at the heart of religion: love, compassion, and justice. Hence, the prophet went on to tell them that they should feed the hungry, shelter the homeless, and clothe the naked.

All this has great relevance for us. Most of us undertake some penance for Lent. This is a good and worthwhile practice. However, penance is not an end in itself. The object of penance is, firstly, to help us reform a sinful way of life, and secondly, to make us more just and more compassionate in our dealings with others.

REFLECTION — *Effective penance*

There was a man who decided to gave up smoking and to go to daily Mass for Lent. Both of these are praiseworthy things, and not easy either. But to what effect?

The man is well known for his impatience. As Lent went on he became so short-tempered that he was impossible to live with. At the end of it everybody was relieved when he went back to his cigarettes.

He is also a very judgemental person. Did going to daily Mass cause him to look at the kind of judgements he was making about other people? Not a bit.

And he is also known as being a very selfish person. Did his Lenten observances make him less selfish? Not a bit.

The Lord might say to that man the sort of things he said to the Israelites through the prophet Isaiah: 'Is this the kind of penance I want? To see you go around looking miserable and making life unbearable for others? To see you honour me in church while you continue to dishonour me in others? To see you appear to be self-sacrificing while you refuse to share with others?

'I'll tell you the kind of penance that pleases me. Make life easier for those who live under the same roof as you. Guard your tongue when you are tempted to speak unkindly of others. Be friendly towards others, especially someone you don't normally mix with or particularly like.'

The truth is: we are far more willing to take on outward penances, even difficult ones, rather than undertake the more necessary and difficult task of changing ourselves. But in calling on us to change what is wrong in our lives, God is calling us to a more joyful and fruitful life. If we live as God wants us to live, then the light of our goodness will shine for all to see. And we will experience the joy of God's presence in your lives.

REFLECTION — *Seeking God*

The people to whom the First Reading was addressed were religious people who sought God, and longed to know his ways. Yet they did not find him. They did not feel that he heard their prayers, or took note of their acts of penance. Why was this? It was because of their sins. Just as dark clouds shut out the sun, so sin shuts out the presence of God.

Hence, the prophet Isaiah was asked by God to proclaim to the people their sins. What sins? 'You do business on your fast days, you oppress your workers, you quarrel and squabble when you fast, you strike the poor man with your fist.'

What the prophet says is also relevant for us. Lent is a time for seeking God – through prayer, fasting, and works of charity. However, no matter how earnestly we pray, or what penances we undertake, we will seek God in vain if we ignore him, or hurt him, or exploit him in our neighbour.

There is a kind of religion which is sterile, self-serving, and has no real influence on our lives. It is a religion which is divorced from a concern for social justice.

Genuine religion is necessarily linked with the practice of justice and concern for the poor and the needy. It involves acting with integrity, treating people fairly, refraining from any form of oppression, sharing with those in need. This is true and authentic religion. This is the way to seek God.

Jesus was sent into the world by the Father to usher in the wedding feast of the Kingdom of God. Yet for all their earnestness and seriousness, the Pharisees failed to recognise him.

It is sad, even tragic, to see people put great effort into their religion, yet miss the heart of it all – love. Nothing can make up for this.

PRAYER OF THE FAITHFUL

Celebrant: Let us bring our needs before God with humble

and contrite hearts.

Response: Lord, graciously hear us.

Reader(s): For Christians: that their worship of God may show itself in the way they treat other people. [Pause] Lord, hear us.

For those who hold public office: that they may promote justice for all, but especially for the weaker members of society. [Pause] Lord, hear us.

For those who take their religion seriously but who are blind to their sins against their neighbour. [Pause] Lord, hear us.

For this congregation: that Lent may awaken in us a spirit of self-denial, and move us to help those in need. [Pause] Lord, hear us.

For our own special needs. [Longer pause] Lord, hear us.

Celebrant: Merciful God, through the grace of this holy season, help us to act justly, to love sincerely, and to walk humbly with you. We ask this through Christ our Lord.

PRAYER/REFLECTION

Just as there is no point in planting a seed
if the ground is frozen,
so repentance of itself is not enough;
grace must be available.
Lord, touch our hearts with your grace,
so that we may rid ourselves of sin,
and devote ourselves to the works of love.
Then your light will shine on us,
and we will know the joy of your presence in our lives.

SATURDAY AFTER ASH WEDNESDAY

INTRODUCTION AND CONFITEOR

In today's Gospel we see Jesus eating and drinking with sinners.

We are gathered around the Lord's table, not because we think we are saints, but because we know we are sinners, sinners who need God's forgiveness and healing. [Pause]

Lord Jesus, you came to heal the broken-hearted. Lord, have mercy.

You came to call sinners to repentance. Christ, have mercy.

You came to seek out and to save the lost. Lord, have mercy.

SCRIPTURE NOTE

The *First Reading* (Is 59:9-14) is a continuation of yesterday's reading. Isaiah makes it clear that genuine worship of God must involve, firstly, a turning away from evil, and secondly, the practice of justice and concern for the poor and the needy. The prophet outlines a pattern of living which, if followed, will result in holiness and happiness.

In the *Gospel* (Lk 5:27-32) we see how Jesus scandalised the Scribes and Pharisees by eating and drinking with people who did not observe the dietary laws or the laws concerning ritual cleanness which were regarded as equally binding as the Law itself. The Pharisees regarded such people as sinners, and avoided social contact with them. Chief among these were tax collectors. Tax collectors were banned from the synagogue and treated as the dregs of society.

Jesus didn't deny that they were sinners. But he said that it was to call sinners that he had come. Just as a doctor devotes his time not to the healthy but to the sick, so he had come to call not the virtuous people but sinners to repentance. Sinners would be healed, not by shunning them, but by caring for them.

REFLECTION — *He mixed with sinners*

The Pharisees would have nothing to do with sinners. According to them, sinners were cursed by God, and therefore beyond redemption.

Jesus, on the other hand, mixed with sinners. It was not a question of a few kind words, or a gesture or two, on his part. He associated with sinners. He shared their food and drink. He put them at ease by his words, but especially by his attitude towards them. Not surprisingly many responded to him and changed their lives.

Jesus distinguished between the sinner and the sin. He condemned the sin but forgave the sinner. He saw sinners as members of God's family, wounded members, but still members.

It would have been easier and more popular for him to go among the good. But he wasn't thinking of himself. He was thinking of others, and of the mission given him by his Father. That mission was to seek out and save the sheep that were lost.

If we are sinners – and which of us is not a sinner? – then Christ loves us not less but more. It doesn't do us much good to be loved for being perfect. We need to be accepted and loved precisely as sinners.

Christ, who sat down at Levi's table, now (in the Eucharist) invites us to sit at his table, in order that he may tend our wounds and nourish us.

Then, as sinners, who have experienced the love of Christ, we must strive to become ministers of his mercy and compassion to others. This, and not penance, is what the Lord desires from us.

REFLECTION — *Your light will shine*

The prophet Isaiah told the people that genuine worship of God must involve, firstly, a turning away from evil, and secondly, the practice of justice and concern for the poor and the needy. He went on to outline a pattern of living which, if followed, will cause God's light to shine on them.

Alas, we disciples of Jesus sometimes walk in darkness. To do an unjust deed, a hurtful deed, is to be in the dark. But we must not despair. We look to the example of Jesus. He didn't shun sinners. He befriended them, and led them out of darkness into the light.

However, it is not enough for us just to avoid doing evil. We must do the good and right deed. When we see that the truth is told, that justice is done, and when we exercise mercy and compassion in our dealings with others, then God's light will shine on us.

The shortest journey to the light is by doing good. We must try to ensure that the light of truth and justice shines in our words and deeds.

The most precious light of all is the light of love. Without that light the world would be a very dark place. Love lights up everything. It brings hope to a world darkened by selfishness, indifference, and hatred.

The image of God is at its best and brightest in us when we love. People who love shed light around them. They are like a lamp alight and shining.

REFLECTION — *The call of Levi*

Levi was a surprising choice on Jesus' part. He was a tax collector. At that time tax collectors were hated by the people – they were seen as collaborators with their foreigners occupiers, the Romans.

But even more surprising was Matthew's immediate and whole-hearted response to the call of Jesus. How do we account for this? It may be that he was finding the job of tax collecting soul destroying. But there must have been positive reasons for his decision to leave everything and follow Jesus.

Deep down inside him was an unfulfilled yearning for goodness. The job of tax collecting was stifling that yearning. So when Jesus offered him a chance to do something better with his life, he grabbed it immediately and with both hands. And a dream, half dead, flared into life.

Still, the decision to follow Jesus can't have been an easy one for him. In meant turning his back on a secure and lucrative job. It meant sacrificing his own plans and ambitions. But he knew that he was being called to a new and more abundant life.

Levi had the courage to answer a call, even though that call subverted all his values. Thus he challenges us. We can learn from so focused on our own goals and schedules that we refuse to be involved in anything that threatens those goals and schedules.

Besides, for all our industry, we may be stagnating. Each of us has a greater possibility. Emerson says, 'There is in each of us a chamber, or a closet, that has never been opened.' If we are to realise this greater possibility, we need to be challenged to go beyond what we think we are capable of or have settled for. The quality of people's lives is affected, not so much by what is given to them, as by what is asked of them.

Jesus' invitation to Levi, 'Follow me', is directed at us also. Lent is an opportunity to respond to that call more wholeheartedly. In is an opportunity to become more committed disciples of Jesus.

PRAYER OF THE FAITHFUL

Celebrant: Let us now bring our needs before God, who has brought us out of darkness into the wonderful light of his Son.

Response: Lord, graciously hear us.

Reader(s): For the Church: that it may show the compassionate face of Christ to sinners. [Pause] Lord, hear us.

For those who make and enforce our laws: that they may do so in a way that does not discriminate against the poor. [Pause] Lord, hear us.

For the sick: that they may experience the love of Christ through the service of those who care for them. [Pause] Lord, hear us.

For all in this congregation: that we may grow in closeness to Christ, the friend of sinners. [Pause] Lord, hear us.

For our own special needs. [Longer pause] Lord, hear us.

Celebrant: Heavenly Father, shed your light into our hearts, so that we may rid ourselves of the works of darkness, and walk in the light of truth and goodness. We make this prayer through Christ our Lord.

PRAYER/REFLECTION

Lent is the Church's 'holy spring'.
Even though it is a time of self-denial,
it is also a time of joy,
because we are preparing for Easter.
Lord, help us to let go of old habits of sin,
and clothe us in newness of life,
so that when Easter comes,
we will feel young again in our discipleship.

First Week of Lent

MONDAY OF FIRST WEEK OF LENT

INTRODUCTION AND CONFITEOR

As disciples of Jesus we are called to holiness. However, today's scripture readings make clear that there can be no holiness for us without concern for our neighbour. Let us reflect on this for a moment. [Pause]

Lord Jesus, you teach us how to love God with all our heart and all our soul. Lord, have mercy.

You teach us how to love our neighbour as ourselves. Christ, have mercy.

You teach us that these two commandments sum up the whole of religion. Lord, have mercy.

SCRIPTURE NOTE

The *First Reading* (Lev 9:1-2.11-18) is concerned with the responsibility to practise justice and charity in our dealings with our neighbour. The influence of the Decalogue is clearly evident. Since God is holy, we are to be holy. But there can be no holiness without love of neighbour.

Love of neighbour entails refraining from harming our neighbour in any way. It also precludes a spirit of envy, revenge, and grudge-bearing, and requires that fraternal correction be made when necessary. In Leviticus the commandment: 'You must love your neighbour as yourself' is restricted to fellow-Israelites. But Jesus broadened it to include everyone.

Love of neighbour is also the theme of the *Gospel* (Mt 25:31-46). This stresses the primacy of love in the life of a Christian. We don't know how the Last Judgement will happen, but we do know what the followers of Jesus will be judged on. They will be judged on love. Or more precisely, on the love they have shown, or refused to show, to the poor and the needy.

REFLECTION — *How to save ourselves*

We don't know how the Last Judgement will happen, but we do know what the followers of Jesus will be judged on. They will be judged on love they have shown, or refused to show, to the poor and the needy.

Once a sailor got stranded on a desert island and soon abandoned hope of escaping from it. However, as a last resort, he placed a message in a bottle which he threw into the sea as the tide was retreating.

One day about a month later he was walking along the beach when he came upon a bottle lying at the water's edge. Inside the bottle he found a message. The message was almost identical to the one he himself had written. It was from a sailor marooned on an island.

'There's nothing I can do about it,' he exclaimed. But just as he was about to throw the piece of paper away, he considered more carefully the location of the island as described in the note. It was due east of where he was, and not all that far away. So he said to himself, 'Maybe I can do something to help, after all.'

That afternoon he started to build a raft. It was only a makeshift affair, crafted out of bamboos, and held together by strands of grass. Nevertheless, a couple of days later, when the currents and the tide were favourable, with a prayer in his heart he launched the raft into the sea, and headed east.

On the morning of the third day, a speck of land appeared on the horizon. That evening he stepped ashore on the island where he was embraced by the other sailor. After a couple of days rest, together they decided to build a larger and better raft. When it was finished they set sail. And, miraculously, a few days later they were rescued by a passing ship.

In saving others, we save ourselves.

REFLECTION — *Sins of omission*

Reflecting on his experience in Auschwitz, the Italian writer, Primo Levi, said, 'Few survivors feel guilty about having deliberately robbed or beaten a companion, but almost everyone feels guilty of having omitted to help a companion who was weaker.'

One day he and a companion were working in a cellar without ventilation, and were dying of thirst. He managed to tap a pipe which ran through the cellar and got a glassful of water out of it. However, instead of sharing it with his companion, he drank it all himself. Afterwards whenever he recalled that unshared glass of water he felt ashamed of himself.

In the judgement scene, people are condemned by the King, not because of evil they did, but because of good they failed to do – 'I was hungry and you gave me nothing to eat.' They are condemned, not for sins of *commission,* but for sins of *omission.*

When we examine our conscience prior to going to Confession, we usually ask ourselves, 'What sins have I committed?' We rarely look at our sins of omission, which may well be our worst sins. We may think we are good simply because we don't do anyone any harm. But what about the good we fail to do?

From a Christian point of view, there is only one real failure in life – the failure to love. If one's love is active, failure to reach perfection in other areas of one's life will be forgiven. But there is no substitute for active love.

Hence, we should concentrate on doing good, rather than on merely avoiding evil. Let us not wait for big opportunities. Let us avail of the little opportunities that come our way every day – opportunities to be friendly, to be helpful, to be considerate, to be obliging …

Genuinely good people hardly realise they are doing good, and have to be reminded of it – 'When did we see you hungry?' They have reached that happy state where giving has become second nature to them.

REFLECTION — *The nothing people*

It is said that there is only one real failure for a Christian – the failure to love. In the judgement scene, people are condemned by the King, not because of evil they did, but because of good they failed to do – 'I was hungry and you gave me nothing to eat.' They are condemned, not for sins of *commission,* but for sins of *omission.*

When we examine our conscience prior to going to confession, we rarely look at our sins of omission. Yet these may well be our worst sins. We may think we are good simply because we don't do anyone any harm. But what about the good we fail to do? There is a reflection entitled 'The Nothing People' which goes like this:

'They do not lie; they merely neglect to tell the truth.

They do not take; they merely can't bring themselves to give.

They will not rock the boat; they merely refuse to pull an oar.

They will not pull you down; they merely won't lend a hand to raise you up.

They do not hurt you; they merely will not help you.

They do not hate you; they merely will not love you.

They are the nothing people, the sins-of-omission people; neither hot nor cold – just lukewarm.

Lord, let me be a saint, or even an honest sinner.

But save me from being a nothing person.'

Sometimes you hear people say, 'I haven't done anyone any

harm.' They seem to regard this as the highest criterion of virtue. But it is a negative criterion. Jesus had a different criterion. It consisted not merely in avoiding evil but in doing good.

In exhorting us to open their hearts to others, Jesus is not laying a burden on us. He is calling us to life, for to open one's heart is to begin to live. Let us not wait for big opportunities. Let us avail of the little opportunities that come our way every day – opportunities to be friendly, to be helpful, to be considerate, to be obliging …

PRAYER OF THE FAITHFUL

Celebrant: Let us pray that the disciples of Jesus may live by the commandment of love.

Response: Lord, hear us in your love.

Reader(s): For Christians: that they may be an example to the world by the love they show for one another. [Pause] We pray in faith.

For government leaders: that as they work to build the earthly city, they may not lose sight of the heavenly kingdom. [Pause] We pray in faith.

For the poor of the world: that they may experience the love of Christ through the care and concern shown them by his followers. [Pause] We pray in faith.

For grace to be sensitive to the needs of others. [Pause] We pray in faith.

For our own special needs. [Longer pause] We pray in faith.

Celebrant: God of love and mercy, your Son so loved the world that he gave his life for us. May we have the courage to live by that same love. We ask this through the same Christ our Lord.

REFLECTION

Religion should not make life burdensome.
If Jesus placed any burden on us,
it was that of loving one another.
But in exhorting us to love one another,

he is not laying a burden on us.
Rather, he is calling us to life,
for to open our heart is to begin to live.
The only real failure in the life of a Christian
is the failure to love.

TUESDAY OF FIRST WEEK OF LENT

INTRODUCTION AND CONFITEOR

Prayer and faith are closely connected. It is because we have
faith that we pray. At the same time prayer sustains our faith. We
need to pray, not just when we are in trouble, but at all times.
Let us turn to God now. [Pause]

Lord Jesus, you are the source of our help. Lord, have mercy.

You keep our feet from stumbling and our hearts from stray-
ing. Christ, have mercy.

You guard our coming and going both now and for ever. Lord,
have mercy.

SCRIPTURE NOTE

The *First Reading* (Is 55:10-11) says that just as God cares for
the earth by sending rain to make it fruitful, he cares for us by
sending us his word. The reading stresses the power and effectiveness of the word of God. The rain always produces positive
results; eventually somewhere the earth responds and becomes
fruitful. So God persists with his word until he gets a response.

In the *Gospel* (Mt 6:7-15) Jesus urges us to pray to God with
childlike trust. The lengthy recital of our needs is discouraged
on the grounds that God already knows them. This is followed
by the Lord's Prayer. This is contrasted with pagan prayer, which
is dismissed as 'babbling'. There may be an allusion here to the
long and tedious magical formulas in which meaningless epi-
thets were piled up.

Matthew's version of the Lord's Prayer has seven petitions.

The first three petitions are really synonymous; they express the desire for the escathological realisation of the kingdom. The other petitions are concerned with our temporal and spiritual needs: daily sustenance, forgiveness of our sins, victory over temptation (trial), and deliverance from evil.

Verses 14 and 15 are a commentary on the petition for forgiveness; they emphasise the duty of forgiveness as a condition for receiving forgiveness.

REFLECTION — *Reflecting on the Lord's Prayer*

The Lord's Prayer is the greatest of all Christian prayers. Properly understood, it contains a whole programme for Christian living.

The first part deals with our relationship with God.

We begin by acknowledging God's existence, and calling him 'Father'. God is a parent to us, and we are his children.

Then we praise his name. In praising God's name we praise God.

We pray for the coming of God's kingdom – a kingdom of truth and life, holiness and grace, justice, love, and peace. We have a part to play in making that kingdom a reality.

We pray that God's will may be done on earth. 'On earth' means in our lives too. God's will may not always be the easiest thing to do, but it is always the best thing.

The second part deals with us and our needs.

We begin by praying for our daily bread. 'Bread' stands for all our material needs. All we really need is enough for today.

We pray for forgiveness for our own sins, and for the grace to be able to forgive those who sin against us. These two things are intimately connected. Inability to forgive others makes it impossible for us to receive God's forgiveness.

We pray not to be led into temptation. God does not put temptation in our path but life does. And we ourselves sometimes walk into temptation of our own accord. We are asking God to help us to cope with the temptations that come to us unbidden, and to avoid those of our own choosing.

Finally, we pray to be delivered from evil. Once again we can't expect never to encounter evil. We are asking God's help so that we may overcome all evil.

Notice that the whole of the Lord's Prayer is couched in plural terms. This shows that we are one family under God, and that there can be no salvation for us independent of others.

(On reaching the Our Father in the Mass, we might ask the congregation to slow it down so as to reflect on its meaning.)

REFLECTION — *Slowing down the Lord's Prayer*

The Lord's Prayer is the first and greatest of all Christian prayers. Properly understood, it contains a whole programme for Christian living.

Unfortunately, like all prayers, it suffers from repetition. It tends to be said hurriedly and unthinkingly so that much of its meaning is lost. We need to slow it down, think about the meaning of what we are saying and its implications for our lives. Above all, we have to *pray* it, and not merely *say* it. Often we say prayers rather than pray.

The first part deals with our relationship with God. We acknowledging God's existence, and call him 'Father'. We praise his name. We pray for the coming of his kingdom, and that his will may be done on earth.

The second part deals with us and our needs. We begin by praying for our daily bread, which stands for all our material needs. We pray for forgiveness for our own sins, and for the grace to be able to forgive those who sin against us. We pray for the grace to be able to overcome all the temptations that come to us, bidden and unbidden. Finally we pray for the strength to be able to overcome all evil.

The Our Father lists the essentials themes of prayer: reverence for God and acknowledgement of his holiness; praying for the kingdom to be established where God's will is accomplished; praying for our daily needs; asking for forgiveness, and understanding our own need to forgive others; asking for help in the choices that confront us every day between good and evil; then the final plea for deliverance from the evil influences that surround us. In the 'Our Father' Jesus has given us a simple prayer that covers all the bases.

(On reaching the Our Father in the Mass, we might ask the congregation to slow it down so as to reflect on its meaning.)

REFLECTION — *Short prayers*

Today many people live such busy lives that they have difficulty finding time for prayer. Hence, the advice Jesus gives in today's Gospel is very relevant.

There he discourages the lengthy recital of our needs on the grounds that God already knows them. He says, 'In your prayers do not babble as the pagans do, for they think that by using many words they will make themselves heard. Do not be like them; your heavenly Father knows what you need even before you ask him.' In other words, keep it short and keep it simple.

One of the shortest prayers ever written was written by a French sailor. It goes like this: 'Lord my boat is small and the ocean is great.' It is so short that some have difficulty in believing it is a prayer at all. Not only is it a prayer; it is a great prayer. Even though it appears to say very little, in reality it says everything.

Jesus himself gave us an excellent example of a short pray in the prayer he put into the mouth of the tax collector, who simply knelt before God, beat his breast and said, 'Lord, be merciful to me a sinner.' This short but heart-felt prayer won favour with God.

Another marvellous example of a short and effective prayer is the prayer of the repentant thief: 'Lord, remember me when you come into your kingdom.' That's all he said. But it won him, not only forgiveness, but heaven itself.

In today's Gospel we have another, if slightly longer, example. The 'Our Father' lists the essentials themes of prayer. revelence for God and acknowledgement of his holiness; praying for the kingdom to be established where God's will is accomplished; praying to God for our daily needs; asking for forgiveness, and understanding our own need to forgive others; asking for help in the choices between good and evil that confront us every day; then the final plea for deliverance from the evil influences that surround us. In the 'Our Father' Jesus has given us a simple prayer that covers all the bases.

REFLECTION — *Recitation of the Our Father*

Celebrant: Let us take it a phrase at a time. I will introduce each phrase, then we will say the phrase together.

Celebrant: When our faith is weak, Lord, teach us to pray:

All: Our Father who art in heaven.

C. When we are inclined to forget about you, Lord, teach us to pray:

A. Hallowed be thy name.

C. When we feel pessimistic about our lives and about the state of the world, Lord, teach us to pray:

A. Thy Kingdom come.

C. When we have difficult decisions to make, and are tempted to take the easy way out, Lord, teach us to pray:

A. Thy will be done on earth as it is in heaven.

C. When we complain about little upsets and forget that millions of people are poor and hungry, Lord, teach us to pray:

A. Give us this day our daily bread.

C. When we are worried about our sins, and find it hard to forgive those who sin against us, Lord, teach us to pray:

A. Forgive us our trespasses as we forgive those who trespass against us.

C. When we are troubled by temptation, Lord, teach us to pray:

A. Lead us not into temptation.

C. When we are finding it hard to cope, Lord, teach us to pray:

A. Deliver us from evil.

C. When we are preoccupied with ourselves and our own glory, Lord, teach us to pray:

A. For the Kingdom, the power, and the glory are yours, now and for ever.

> *(If this is to be used, the congregation would*
> *really need copies of the script.)*

PRAYER OF THE FAITHFUL

Celebrant: Let us pray to God in the spirit of the great prayer that Jesus taught us.

Response: Lord, hear our prayer.

Reader(s): That the followers of Jesus may seek to know the will of God and do it. [Pause] Let us pray to the Lord.

That all those responsible for public order may work for the coming of the Kingdom of God. [Pause] Let us pray to the Lord.

That those who are hungry may be given daily bread. [Pause] Let us pray to the Lord.

That, as we pray for forgiveness for our own sins, we may be willing to forgive those who sin against us. [Pause] Let us pray to the Lord.

That we may be given grace to resist temptation and to be victorious over evil. [Pause] Let us pray to the Lord.

For our own special needs. [Longer pause] Let us pray to the Lord.

Celebrant: Heavenly Father, grant that no matter what happens to us, we may never forget that we are your children, and never doubt your love for us. We ask this through Christ our Lord.

PRAYER/REFLECTION

The word of God is to the human heart
what a seed is to the earth.
However, just as a seed needs soil,
so the word needs a receptive heart.

Lord, soften our hearts with your grace,
and warm them with your love,
so that the precious seed of your word
may take root in our hearts,
and bear fruit in our lives.

WEDNESDAY OF FIRST WEEK OF LENT

INTRODUCTION AND CONFITEOR

Today's scripture readings deal with one of the great themes of Lent, namely, repentance. We begin every Mass by calling to mind our sins, and asking God to help us to repent of them. Let us do that now. [Pause]

Lord Jesus, you blot out our sins. Lord, have mercy.
You give us the joy of your help. Christ, have mercy.
You put a steadfast spirit within us. Lord, have mercy.

SCRIPTURE NOTE

Repentance is the main theme of today's readings. The *First Reading* (Jon 3:1-10) provides us with a wonderful example of repentance. It tells how the preaching of Jonah met with a positive response in the pagan city of Nineveh. The people recognised in his voice the voice of God, and undertook to reform their lives, the king himself setting the example. The story also illustrates God's readiness to show mercy, even to Gentiles.

The Ninevites didn't ask for a sign. They accepted Jonah as a messenger from God and repented. In contrast, Jesus' contemporaries refuse to repent at his preaching (*Gospel*, Lk 11:29-32). Instead, they ask for a sign that he was the emissary of God he claimed to be. He told them that the only proof of his credentials he would give them was that which Jonah gave to the Ninevites, namely, a call to repentance issued in the name of God.

Jesus called the Jews of his time 'an evil generation' because, for all their religiosity, they could not recognise the voice of God when they heard it. On judgement day, foreigners like the Queen of the South and the Ninevites would rise up and condemn the Jews of Jesus' time, because these Jews had an opportunity and a privilege far beyond anything they had ever had, yet refused to accept it.

Jesus possessed a wisdom greater even than that of Solomon. And his voice was a more authoritative voice than that of Jonah.

All of this is relevant for us. If the Ninevites responded to the preaching of Jonah, how much more should we respond to the preaching of Jesus.

REFLECTION — *The purpose of penance*

Lent is a time for doing penance. What is the purpose of penance?

The first thing we are doing when we undertake penance is acknowledging that we are sinners, sinners who need God's mercy.

The second thing we are doing is expressing the desire and will to change our lives. The whole object of penance is to reform a sinful way of life.

Penance is an exercise in saying 'no' to ourselves. It is intended to show that we are capable of better things, and that we sincerely want those things. We want to reform our lives, but we know we cannot do so without the grace of God.

When people prune a fruit tree, they are not doing it to hurt the tree, but to make it more fruitful. So our penances have as their goal to lead us to a new and better life.

We see a fine example of this in the First Reading. At the preaching of Jonah the people of Nineveh fasted, put on sackcloth, and prayed earnestly to God. But they didn't leave it at that. Their King urged them to go further. He said, 'Let everyone renounce his evil behaviour and the wicked things he has done.'

It is a lot easier to undertake penances, even severe ones,

than to try to change sinful attitudes, habits, etc. For our penance to bear fruit it must result in a sincere effort to change our lives.

Generally speaking, we will change everything but what counts in our lives. We will adjust, but not too much. We will change only if the changes do not discomfort us or cost us too dearly.

What is the chief thing, or the chief area of my life, that I most need to change? [Pause].

REFLECTION — *Clothing ourselves in newness of life*

Once a king was walking through the streets of the capital city when he came upon a beggar, who asked him for money. The king didn't give him any money. Instead, he invited him to visit him in his palace. The beggar took up the king's offer.

On the appointed day he made his way to the royal palace, and was duly ushered into the king's presence. However, as he came into the king's presence, he became acutely conscious of his rags and felt ashamed of them. Those rags were an eloquent symbol of the misery and wretchedness of his life.

The king, an exceptionally kind man, received him warmly, took pity on him, and among other things gave him a new suit of clothes. However, a few days later the beggar was back begging on the streets dressed in his old rags.

Why did he give up the new suit? Because he knew that if he wore it, he would have to give up the life of a beggar, and make a new life for himself. This he was not prepared to do. It wasn't that the new life didn't appeal to him. It was just that he knew that a change of life would be painful.

In his love for us, God is continually us to a deeper and more authentic life. We may not be guilty of great evil, yet we could be very selfish, very demanding, very inconsiderate. But we don't want to know, much less do anything about this side of our nature.

Yet conversion is a joyful thing. It is a call from the slavery of sin to a life of freedom and grace. It is a call from a life of barrenness to a life of fruitfulness. However, it is not something that is achieved once and for all. It involves a process of growth and development.

We must ask the Lord to help us to let go of the rags of sin, so that he may clothe us in newness of life.

REFLECTION — *The blessings that surround us*

People who go to New York for the first time invariably want to see the Statue of Liberty. They would almost feel they had never been there if they didn't see that. Yet there are people who were born and bred in New York, who have never visited it, nor felt any great desire to do so.

Why is this? Closeness blinds. The nearer a thing is, the harder it is to see it. Familiarity may not always breed contempt, but it invariably breeds indifference. A thing may be under our nose, but if we are indifferent to it, we won't pay attention to it.

The same thing happens with regard to people. The people we are most apt to take for granted are the people with whom we share our lives every day. We make a fuss over a visitor, but neglect our family.

If we fail to appreciate and benefit from the things and the people that surround us, we will cut ourselves off from our main source of nourishment. A tree draws its nourishment from its immediate environment.

Jesus blamed his contemporaries for not believing in him as a messenger sent by God to call them to repentance. He contrasted them with the Queen of the South; she came a long way to hear the wisdom of Solomon. He possessed a wisdom greater than that of Solomon, yet they refused to listen to him.

And he contrasted them with the people of Nineveh; they listened to the preaching of Jonah, and repented. His credentials were greater than the credentials of Jonah, yet they refused to repent at his preaching.

All of this is relevant for us. In Lent, we hear the voice of Jesus calling us to repentance. If the Ninevites responded to the preaching of Jonah, how much more should we respond to the preaching of Jesus.

PRAYER OF THE FAITHFUL

Celebrant: Let us bring our petitions before the Lord with humble and contrite hearts.

Response: Lord, graciously hear us.

Reader(s): For all Christians: that the penances they have undertaken for Lent may make them better disciples of Jesus. [Pause] Lord, hear us.

For those who are blind to their sins, and who see no need to change their lives. [Pause] Lord, hear us.

For the courage to acknowledge what needs to be changed in our lives, and for the will to do something about it. [Pause] Lord, hear us.

For the wisdom to recognise and avail of the opportunities and blessings God sends us each day. [Pause] Lord, hear us.

For our own special needs. [Longer pause] Lord, hear us.

Celebrant: Lord, in your gentle mercy, guide our wayward hearts, for we know that left to ourselves we cannot do your will. We make our prayers through Christ our Lord.

PRAYER / REFLECTION

Sometimes I wish my life was easier.
But there are so many things to be done,
so many problems to be solved.
Sometimes I want to change other people
but am unwilling to change myself.
Lord, grant me the serenity
to accept the things I cannot change,
the courage to change the things I can,
and the wisdom to know the difference.

THURSDAY OF FIRST WEEK OF LENT

INTRODUCTION AND CONFITEOR

Prayer is an essential element of our Lenten observance. Jesus urges us to pray to God with confidence and persistence in all our needs. Let us turn to God now, and ask forgiveness for our sins with confidence and trust. [Pause]

Lord Jesus, you are slow to anger, abounding in love. Lord, have mercy.

You support all who fall, and raise up all who are bowed down. Christ, have mercy.

Though father and mother forsake us, you will receive us. Lord, have mercy.

SCRIPTURE NOTE

Esther (*First Reading* Esth 4:17) was a Jewish maiden married to the Persian King who ruled Israel at that time. The Jews refused to be assimilated and so were seen as a threat to the king's authority. The King issued a decree that all Jews were to be put to death. Since Esther was so close to the King, it fell to her to appeal to him on behalf of her fellow Jews.

Before making her appeal she prayed earnestly to God. Her prayer, which we find in part in the First Reading, was one of desperation but great trust too. She asked God to remember his covenant with Israel, and to come to the aid of his people in their time of peril. For herself she asked only for courage and words that would persuade the king to cancel his decree. Happily, her request was successful and resulted in the salvation of her people.

Intercessory prayer is also the theme of the *Gospel* (Mt 7:7-12). Jesus urges the disciples to pray to God with trust, and to go on asking for what they need with persistence and confidence. He also urges them to imitate God's goodness in their dealings with one another.

REFLECTION — *Prayer of desperation*

An elderly woman, who was having trouble with one of her eyes, went to see a doctor. The doctor, a good man but an unbeliever, discovered that she had a tumour behind the eye. Reluctant to tell her the bad news directly, he asked if he could speak to her husband. She told him she didn't have a husband. Then he asked if he could speak to her children. She told him she had no children.

The doctor was at a loss as to what to say, but she came to his rescue. She said, 'I'm on my own, doctor. Tell me what it is. If the news is bad, it will give me a chance to exercise my faith.'

This woman reminds us a little of Esther. Esther was a Jewish maiden married to the Persian King who ruled Israel at that time. The King issued a decree that all Jews were to be put to death. Since Esther was so close to the King, it fell to her to appeal to him to cancel his decree.

It was a desperate situation for her and for her people. Everything depended on the success of her appeal. Before making that appeal she prayed earnestly to God. Her prayer (which we find in part in the First Reading) was one of desperation but of great trust too:

'O God, my King, come to my help, for I am alone and have no helper but you. I have been taught from my earliest years that you have chosen Israel to be your heritage for ever. Remember us now, Lord, in this time of distress.'

She was praying not for herself but for her people. Her appeal resulted in the salvation of her people.

Any of us could reach a point of desperation in life, and so can make Esther's prayer our own. In the end, our hope lies in God alone. 'I said my prayers every day in Auschwitz' (Elie Wiesel, Auschwitz survivor and Nobel Peace Prize Winner).

REFLECTION — *Ask, seek, knock*

Esther was a Jewish maiden married to the Persian King who ruled Israel at that time. The King issued a decree that all Jews were to be put to death. Since Esther was so close to the King, it fell to her to appeal to him to cancel his decree. Everything depended on the success of her appeal. It was a desperate situation to be in.

Before making that appeal Esther prayed earnestly to God. Her prayer is found in part in the First Reading. She was appealing, not for herself, but for her people. Fortunately, her appeal was successful and the king spared her people.

Her prayer is a model. Though it was one of desperation, it was one of great trust too. It implied courage, trust, and great love. And it impelled her to action.

Many people feel like that at some point in life. There are times when we feel all alone, and that there is no one who really cares or understands. But those who have faith know that they are never alone. They know that God is always with them.

Jesus urges us to have great trust in God. If we, sinful human beings that we are, know how to care for our children, giving them what they need, then how much more will God, whose love far surpasses anything we are capable of, do the same for us. God may not always give us what we *want*. But he will always give us what we *need* in a particular situation.

However, we must not sit back and expect it to fall into our lap. We must actively seek it. God won't do for us what we are unwilling to do for ourselves. Jesus says: 'Ask, seek, and knock.' He is telling us that we must be prepared to ask for it with persistence, and to search for it unflaggingly. An attitude like this always produces results. 'More things are wrought by prayer than this world dreams of' (Tennyson).

REFLECTION — *A stone instead of bread*
What kind of father, asks Jesus, if his son asks for a piece of bread would give him a stone instead? Not much of a father. Not worthy even of the name 'father'. Yet, alas, such things do happen.

A child comes looking for the bread of love, and gets the

stone of rejection.

A teenager comes looking for the bread of understanding, and gets the stone of a reprimand.

A slow pupil comes looking for the bread of encouragement, and gets the stone of a burst of impatience.

A troublesome youth comes looking for the bread of attention, and gets the stone of judgement.

A tired wife comes looking for the bread of appreciation, and gets a stony silence.

A tired husband comes looking for the bread of peace, and gets the stone of constant nagging.

A lonely person comes looking for the bread of companionship, and gets the stone of dismissal.

A concerned, community-minded person comes looking for the bread of funds, and gets the stone of an empty promise from the authorities.

And so it goes on.

Whatever is hateful to ourselves, we should not do to our neighbour. May the Lord forgive us for the times when people came to us looking for bread and we gave them a stone instead. We tend to treat others *as they treat us*. But Jesus says to us is: 'Treat others *as you would like them to treat you.'* Undoubtedly we would like them to give us bread if we asked for bread.

PRAYER OF THE FAITHFUL

Celebrant: Let us bring our needs before our heavenly Father with confidence and trust as Jesus has taught us.

Response: Lord, hear our prayer.

Reader(s): For the followers of Jesus: that they may practise the golden rule. [Pause] Let us pray to the Lord.

For temporal rulers: that they may exercise their authority in a responsible and caring manner. [Pause] Let us pray to the Lord.

For those who are alone and fearful. [Pause] Let us pray to the Lord.

For all gathered here: that we may never doubt God's presence with us in all our trials. [Pause] Let us pray to the Lord.

For grace to show to others the generosity of heart we would like them to show to us. [Pause] Let us pray to the Lord.

For our own special needs. [Longer pause] Let us pray to the Lord.

Celebrant: Heavenly Father, teach us to go on confidently asking, to go on joyfully seeking, and to go on hopefully knocking at the door, so that the good things you want to give us may be ours. We make our prayer through Christ our Lord.

INTRODUCTION TO THE OUR FATHER

Jesus says: 'If you know how to give your children what is good, how much more will your Father in heaven give good things to those who ask him.' Let us pray to our heavenly Father as Jesus taught us.

PRAYER / REFLECTION

Jesus urges us to ask, seek, and knock.
But sometimes we are too proud to ask, so we don't receive;
we are too lazy to seek, so we don't find;
and we are too timid to knock,
so the door doesn't open to us.
Lord, help us to be bold and energetic,
yet humble and trustful,
so that we may receive the good things
which our heavenly Father wants us to have.

FRIDAY OF FIRST WEEK OF LENT

INTRODUCTION AND CONFITEOR

As we approach the altar of the Lord, we recall the words of Jesus: 'If you are bringing your offering to the altar and there remember that your brother has something against you, leave your offering there before the altar, go and be reconciled with your brother first, and then come back and present your offering.' Let us reflect on these words for a moment to see if they apply to us. [Pause]

Lord Jesus, you came to reconcile us to one another and to the Father. Lord, have mercy.

You heal the wounds of sin and division. Christ, have mercy.

You intercede for us at the right hand of the Father. Lord, have mercy.

SCRIPTURE NOTE

In the *First Reading* (Ezek 18:21-28) Ezekiel is responding to an objection that God is unjust because he punishes or rewards the individual for his own actions instead of allowing him to rely on the institution of Israel and the promises made to the nation. The prophet tells them that each individual is responsible for his/her own actions, and will be judged accordingly.

Although the principle of individual responsibility didn't originate with Ezekiel, he gave it its clearest formulation. But he goes on to state that repentance will win the individual pardon and life. What the Lord wants is not the death of the sinner but that he/she should repent and live.

In the *Gospel* (Mt 5:20-26) Jesus proposes new standards of goodness for his disciples. They are not to become better Pharisees. Their virtue must go deeper than the virtue of the Scribes and Pharisees. We are given one example. It concerns the fifth commandment. Jesus reinterprets the commandment 'Thou shalt not kill' so that it embraces those angry feelings and emotions which may lead up to murder. He goes on to make a strong recommendation of fraternal reconciliation, and warns that an unforgiving spirit will come between us and the God we worship.

REFLECTION — *A deeper virtue*

In our culture the image is everything. Appearances are more important than the substance. But appearances can be deceptive. A nut may have a large shell, and yet be empty inside.

Jesus was able to see beneath the appearance to the inner person. And to him it was the inner person that mattered. This brought him into conflict with the Scribes and Pharisees.

He wasn't taken in by their pious exterior. Piety is no substitute for goodness. He had some hard things to say about them. For instance, he compared them to whitewashed tombs. From the outside they appeared to be upright people, but inside they were full of hypocrisy and lawlessness (Mt 23:27-28).

However, the chief fault he found in them was that they lacked charity. For all their piety, they were cold-hearted. If one's heart is cold, how can one be virtuous? He also made a stinging indictment of their worship when he said, 'You honour God with your lips, but your hearts are far from him' (Mt 15:8).

He made it clear that his disciples would have to do better. To them he said, 'If your virtue goes no deeper than that of the Scribes and Pharisees, you will never enter the kingdom of heaven' – words we find in today's Gospel.

Virtue is not exterior demeanour or conformity to social manners. Genuine virtue is interior, that is, rooted in conviction and desire. It is an expression of the heart and the soul.

When all is said and done it is the heart that matters. A person is what the heart is. Our chief concern, then, must be to get the heart right. If the heart is right, then our deeds will be true and genuine. They will flow from what we are, as naturally as good fruit from a good tree.

REFLECTION — *Handling anger*

Anger is something we all have to deal with. We may have been taught that anger was sinful (one of the seven deadly sins). The first thing that needs to be said is that anger is normal and even healthy. If we love and value ourselves, we will naturally get angry if we are badly treated.

We shouldn't deny our anger or repress it. Repressed anger

is very dangerous, and can result in self-hatred and depression. We shouldn't be afraid to allow ourselves to feel angry. People feel guilty about getting angry. But of itself anger is neither good nor bad morally. It is just a feeling.

When in today's Gospel Jesus says, 'Do not get angry with your brother,' he is not condemning anger in itself. After all, he himself got angry. It is when anger turns into hostility that it becomes dangerous. Hostility rather than anger is the real deadly sin. It leads to deep resentments, negative attitudes, insults, and so on, which are directed at the object of our anger.

When we get angry we should look at the cause of our anger. The cause may lie with ourselves. In which case we have to look at ourselves. We must also try to remove the anger others may have towards us by asking for forgiveness, and making amends.

If the cause lies with another person, we have to look at our relationship with that person. If it lies in some unjust situation, we should try to put that situation right. Anger can be a good thing – it can spur us to put right something that is wrong.

We can't avoid getting angry, but we can avoid acting out our anger. Anger is no resting place. 'Anger in the heart is like a worm in a plant' (Talmud). If our heart is filled with anger, there is no room in it for love. At all costs we must keep love in our hearts. Jesus tells us that we have to seek to be reconciled.

REFLECTION — *Individual responsibility*

Today personal responsibility is being eroded. The whole thrust of modern psychoanalysis seems to be directed at removing responsibility from the individual. Someone else is to blame – one's companions, one's parents, one's environment, and so on.

In the First Reading, Ezekiel is dealing with the problem of personal responsibility. The people were complaining that God is unjust because he punishes or rewards the individual for his own actions, instead of allowing him to rely on the institution of Israel and the promises made to the nation. Ezekiel says we cannot hide behind others. He states clearly and unequivocally that each individual is responsible for his or her actions, and he or she alone will have to answer for them.

We are, of course, influenced by our upbringing and environment. Still, there must come a time when we stop blaming others, and accept responsibility for our actions. We have to say, 'The buck stops with me.' It is refreshing to hear someone say, 'I am to blame. I am responsible.' But how rarely it happens.

Lent provides us with an opportunity to do just this. We are asked to look at our lives, see what is wrong in them, accept responsibility for it, and then try to change it. We have nothing to fear but the mercy of God, for Ezekiel says, 'God does not desire the death of the sinner but that he be converted and live.'

Unless we accept responsibility for our sins, we will see no need to repent of them. If we do accept responsibility for them, we will want to do something about them, and God will help us.

PRAYER OF THE FAITHFUL

Celebrant: Let us with confidence approach God in our needs because with him is mercy and fullness of redemption.

Response: Lord, hear our prayer.

Reader(s): For all followers of Christ: that they may have the kind of relationship with God which makes obeying his commandments natural and easy. [Pause] Let us pray to the Lord.

For those who hold public office: that they may be faithful to their responsibilities. [Pause] Let us pray to the Lord.

For all in this congregation: that our virtue may be true and genuine. [Pause] Let us pray to the Lord.

For the wisdom and self-discipline to use our anger positively. [Pause] Let us pray to the Lord.

For our own special needs. [Longer pause] Let us pray to the Lord.

Celebrant: All-powerful God, help us to keep our thoughts clean, our desires pure, our words true, and our deeds kind. We ask this through Christ our Lord.

REFLECTION

Jesus says, 'If you are going to the altar,
and remember that your brother has something against you,
leave your offering there before the altar,
and go and be reconciled with your brother first.'
Sadly, many see no contradiction in going to the altar
without being reconciled with someone they have offended.
We should take the words of Jesus seriously.
We would not go to the altar with dirt on our hands.
Why go there with blackness in our heart?

SATURDAY OF FIRST WEEK OF LENT

INTRODUCTION AND CONFITEOR

Jesus tells us that God loves all of his children, deserving and undeserving. And he urges us to imitate this all-embracing love of God. We know how difficult love can be, especially in relation to people we don't like. [Pause].

Lord Jesus, you care for us as a loving father cares for his children. Lord, have mercy.

You let the sun of your love shine on good people and bad people. Christ, have mercy.

You let the rain of your mercy fall on saints and sinners. Lord, have mercy.

SCRIPTURE NOTE

Moses (*First Reading*, Deut 26:16-19) urges the people to live according to God's commandments, and assures them of God's special favour if they do so. This sounds as if God's love is conditional. But Jesus makes it clear that God's love is unconditional.

In Levitcus, the commandment 'You must love your neighbour as yourself' is restricted to fellow-Israelites. But Jesus (*Gospel*, Mt 5:43-48) broadened it to include Gentiles as well as Jews, and enemies as well as friends. Love within one's group or fellowship is merely a natural and universal human trait. It does not distinguish the Christian from the non-Christian. What makes the disciples of Christ different from other people is their ability to love even their enemies. By this kind of love the disciples will be perfect as the heavenly Father is perfect.

REFLECTION — *Choosing between love and hate*

A native American was talking to his grandson about how he felt about the atrocity that happened in New York City on September 11, 2001. He said, 'I feel as if I have two wolves fighting in my heart. One wolf is angry, vengeful, and violent. The other is loving, forgiving, and compassionate.'

'Which wolf will win the fight in your heart?' the grandson asked him.

'The one I feed,' he answered.

The injunction 'Love your enemy' is a radical rejection of violence. Returning love for hate is one of the most difficult things in the world. It is a very high ideal, and a very difficult one, but it makes sense.

We are not expected to *feel* love for our enemy. Love is not a feeling; it is an act of the will. We can make a decision to love someone, even though we do not have feelings of love for that person.

Jesus' way is not an easy way, but it is a better way. He challenges us to respond to darkness with light. The escalation of evil can be stopped only by one who humbly absorbs it, without passing it on. Revenge and retaliation only add darkness to darkness. Revenge may satisfy a person's rage but it leaves the heart empty.

Our hearts were made to love, not to hate. Love is more beautiful than hate. Hate poisons the heart, but love purifies it. At all costs, then, we must keep love in our heart. The image of God is at its best and brightest in us when we love.

The power of love is greater than the power of evil. Love releases extraordinary energies in us. And love is never lost. If not reciprocated, it will flow back and soften and purify the heart.

REFLECTION — *A better way*

Jesus says to us, 'Love your enemies, and pray for those who persecute you.' Love our enemies! We find it hard enough to love our friends, so how can we be expected to love our enemies?

Jesus is telling us to love, not to hate. Hatred is a very destructive thing. When we hate we expend more energy than in any other emotion. We mustn't dissipate our strength in hating but save it for better things.

This is why Jesus urges us not to have hatred in our hearts for anyone, not even our enemies. It is not only for the sake of the enemy that he says to us, 'Love your enemies', but for our own sake too. Hatred may not destroy its object, but it will surely destroy the one who hates. 'Ten enemies cannot hurt a person as much as he hurts himself' (Proverb).

Jesus never said that we would have no enemies – there is no lack of realism here. But he offers us a new way of dealing with our enemies, a different way of responding that has the potential to break the endless cycle of retaliation that now threatens us all with ultimate violence.

Jesus' way is not an easy way, but it is a better way. He challenges us to respond to darkness with light. The escalation of evil can be stopped only by one who humbly absorbs it, without passing it on. Revenge and retaliation only add darkness to darkness.

Our hearts were made to love, not to hate. Love is more beautiful than hate. Hate poisons the heart, but love purifies it. At all costs, then, we must keep love in our heart. The image of God is at its best and brightest in us when we love.

If we pray for our enemies, peace will come to us. And when we love our enemies, we can be certain that divine grace dwells in us.

REFLECTION — *God's unconditional love*

At the end of a lifetime devoted to teaching boys in a New York high school, a Jesuit priest said: 'Every boy I ever taught was infected with the subconscious conviction that if he didn't succeed he wouldn't be loved.'

It is not surprising then that we tend to expect the same kind of treatment from God. We believe that God will love us only if we are good. But Jesus tells us that God is not like that. He says that God loves all of his children, deserving and undeserving. He lets the sun of his love shine on good people and bad people, and lets the rain of his mercy fall on saints and sinners.

This means that God loves us regardless of whether or not we are worthy of his love. God loves us, not because we are good, but because he is good. Our very existence is a sign of God's love. God's unconditional love for us is the Good News.

Therefore, we do not have to worry about trying to earn his love. All we have to do is open ourselves to receive it. Then maybe we will begin to love others as God loves us. We will not wait to discover good qualities in them before loving them. We will love them without preconditions, and then discover reasons that make them worthy of our love.

Jesus urges us to love even our enemies. This doesn't mean that we have to *feel* love for our enemy. Love is not a feeling; it is an act of the will. To love an enemy goes clean contrary to human nature. Only God can help us to love in the way Jesus asks us to love.

When Jesus asks us to be perfect as our heavenly Father is perfect, the perfection he is talking about is the perfection of love. God loves his children unconditionally. Jesus is urging us to imitate this all-embracing love of God.

PRAYER OF THE FAITHFUL

Celebrant: Let us pray to our heavenly Father who lets his sun shine and his rain fall on all of his children, deserving and undeserving.

Response: Lord, graciously hear us.

Reader(s): For peace and harmony among Christians of different denominations. [Pause] Lord, hear us.

For peace and harmony in countries where the population is made up of different religious and ethnic groups. [Pause] Lord, hear us.

For the healing of relationships that are strained or that have gone sour. [Pause] Lord, hear us.

For those who have hurt us in any way, and whom we find hard to love. [Pause] Lord, hear us.

For our own special needs. [Longer pause] Lord, hear us.

Celebrant: Merciful God, fill our hearts with your love. Give us the grace to rise above our human weakness, and keep us faithful in loving you and one another. We make this prayer through Christ our Lord.

REFLECTION / PRAYER – GIVING
There are those who give
only on condition that they receive something in return,
and receive it immediately.
There are those who give
on condition that they receive something in return,
later on and with a handsome profit.
And there are those who give
without expecting anything in return now or ever.
These are imitating the generosity of God,
who bestows his love on good people and bad,
and grants mercy to saints and sinners.

Second Week of Lent

MONDAY OF SECOND WEEK OF LENT

INTRODUCTION AND CONFITEOR

Jesus said to his disciples: 'Be compassionate ... Do not judge ... Do not condemn.' These words, taken from today's Gospel, are now said to us. Let us call to mind our failures to by live by these words. [Pause] The Lord himself sets us the example.

Lord Jesus, you are slow to anger and rich in mercy. Lord, have mercy.

You do not treat us according to our sins nor repay us according to our faults. Christ, have mercy.

As far as the east is from the west, so far do you remove our sins. Lord, have mercy.

SCRIPTURE NOTE

In the *First Reading* (Dan 9:4-10) the prophet Daniel pleads with God on behalf of the people. He acknowledges the people's sins and the shame they have brought on themselves through their disregard for his commandments and refusal to listen to his prophets. He rests his appeal on the kindness of God to whom mercy and pardon belong.

In the *Gospel* (Lk 6:36-38) Jesus urges his disciples to imitate the kindness and compassion of God. After the injunction to love our enemies (see last Saturday), he goes on to stress the obligations of fraternal charity. He asks us to be compassionate, forgiving, and generous towards one another, and assures us that whatever we give to others will be given back to us with interest.

REFLECTION — *On not judging*

When Jesus tells us not to judge, he is not talking about society as a whole. Society has to have judges and courts. And he is not saying we should abandon our critical faculties. We have to

---

judge between good and evil. He is talking about our ordinary relationships with one another.

I was watching a soccer match on television. When the referee disallowed a goal, I was fully convinced that he had made a mistake. However, when they replayed the incident, showing it through the lens of another camera which had a wider view, it became clear that the referee had got it right after all. The scorer was offside.

Where others are concerned, we seldom see the wider picture, much less the full picture. Even so, it doesn't stop us from jumping to conclusions and rushing to judgement. Even when we do see the whole picture, we still should refrain from hasty judgements. Even then we are still only on the surface; we can't see into people's minds and hearts. We may see the deed, but we can't see the motives behind the deed.

We should therefore refrain from judging other people because we seldom know all the facts. Even when we do, we still have no right to judge them. At some time or other all of us have been the victims of hasty judgements. We know how hurtful this is. When it happens, it makes us hate all judgement.

All of us can say with the prophet Daniel, 'Lord, we have sinned, we have done wrong, we have betrayed your commandments.' Though we deserve God's judgement, which of us wants to receive that judgement? Do we not all long for, and need, God's mercy and forgiveness?

Conscious of our own abhorrence of judgement, we should refrain from judgement altogether. By our judgements we convict ourselves.

REFLECTION — *On generosity*

Jesus says that the amount we measure out to others is the amount that will be given back to us. There was a country which was famous for producing grain. However, not all the farmers were well-off. The king, who was noted for his wisdom and compassion, asked the well-off farmers to share with the poorer ones.

'How much do we have to give?' they asked.

'How much are you willing to give?' said the king in reply.

They went away to think things over. Some thought the king's request a good idea. Some were lukewarm about it. And some were opposed to it. Nevertheless, all felt obliged to give something. The first group gave a sackful each. The second group a bucketful each. And the third group gave a cupful each.

This went on for years. Then one year the harvest failed throughout the land. Everybody was desperate. But the king sent out word that he had grain to distribute. Where had this grain come from? Over the years he had been putting some grain from their donations aside against just such an eventuality.

'How much are we going to get?' they asked the king.

And he replied, 'My friends, those who gave a sackful will get a sackful; those who gave a bucketful will get a bucketful; and those who gave a cupful will get a cupful.'

The vessel with which we give to others is the vessel with which we receive from God. It is not that God is being mean-spirited and vindictive. The fault lies not with God but with us. To give is to open one's heart. The more we open our heart to give, the greater becomes our capacity to receive.

If we are generous towards others, God will see to it that the blessings we bestow will be returned to us, a full measure, pressed down, shaken together, and running over.

REFLECTION — *The values of the kingdom*

Jesus says: 'Be compassionate as your Father is compassionate.' The one thing one would expect to find in a religious person is the virtue of compassion. Without a warm, compassionate heart one cannot call oneself a true human being, never mind a truly religious person.

Then he says, 'Do not judge, and you will not be judged yourselves; do not condemn, and you will not be condemned yourselves.' Society has to have judges and courts. Jesus is not talking about that. He is talking about our ordinary relationships with one another.

Where others are concerned, we never see the full picture. In every person there is a dimension that escapes us. We can't see into the mind and heart of another. Which means we are not in a position to judge. We've all been the victims of hasty and unfair judgements. We know how hurtful that can be.

All of us are sinners, and therefore deserve God's judgement. But what we long for is not judgement but mercy and forgiveness. So, as far as possible, we should refrain from judgement altogether. By our judgements we convict ourselves.

Finally Jesus says, 'Give a full measure, pressed down, shaken together, running over. The amount you measure out is the amount you will be given back.'

He is urging his disciples to be generous with one another. If we are generous we ourselves will benefit too. An open, generous heart is a joyful heart. A miserly heart is a sad heart. Besides, what we give will come back, multiplied many times over. God will see to it that the blessings we bestow will be returned to us, a full measure, pressed down, shaken together, and running over.

Jesus' vision of human behaviour is at such variance with the view most people have, that many people regard it as humanly unachievable, and therefore ignore it. From a human point of view it is unachievable. Divine help is needed.

PRAYER OF THE FAITHFUL

Celebrant: God is kind and compassionate to all his creatures. Therefore, let us bring our needs before him with confidence.

Response: Lord, graciously hear us.

Reader(s): For all Christians: that they may be known for their generosity, compassion, and forgiveness. [Pause] Lord, hear us.

For judges: that they may show wisdom and compassion in the exercise of their office. [Pause] Lord, hear us.

For those who have been the victims of unfair judgements. [Pause] Lord, hear us.

Fro grace to show to others the same kindness and understanding we hope God will show to us. [Pause] Lord, hear us.

For our own special needs. [Longer pause] Lord, hear us.

Celebrant: Lord, grant that we may be more willing to praise than to criticise, to sympathise than to condemn, and to give rather than to receive, so that the world will know that we are disciples of your Son, who lives and reigns with you and the Holy Spirit, one God for ever and ever.

PRAYER / REFLECTION

Jesus urges us to be generous towards others.
And if we are generous towards others,
the blessings we bestow will be returned to us,
multiplied many times over.
To be generous means to open our heart.
The more we open our heart to give,
the greater becomes our capacity to receive.
Blessed are the open-hearted;
they will be able to give *and* to receive.

TUESDAY OF SECOND WEEK OF LENT

INTRODUCTION AND CONFITEOR

Jesus' main criticism of the Scribes and Pharisees was that they didn't practise what they preached. To some extent, all of us fail in this regard. Let us call to mind those failings now. [Pause]

I confess to almighty God …

SCRIPTURE NOTE

The *First Reading* (Is 1:10.16-20) is a call to repentance addressed to the rulers of Sodom and Gomorrah. True repentance involves ceasing to do evil. But it doesn't stop there. It also involves doing good: practising justice, helping the oppressed, pleading for orphans and widows. Complete pardon is prom ised if they heed the call to repentance; disaster awaits them if they don't. This was not meant as a threat. What comes across is God's concern for the inhabitants of the two cities.

In the *Gospel* (Mt 23:1-12) Jesus directs some harsh words at the Scribes and Pharisees. He begins by advising the people and his disciples to follow what they say, because of their historical authority. But on no account should they follow their example, because they don't practice what they preach. They increase the duties of religion for others, but do not live what is at the heart of religion: love, compassion, and justice. They are ostentatious in the performance of religious practices, and look for honour and reward from people in the present rather than from God in the future. The person who is a humble servant in the present, will be exalted by God in the age to come.

The message is as relevant now as it was back then. Christian leaders are in danger of repeating the mistakes of the Pharisees. We are still reluctant to let go of things such as ostentatious dress, places of honour, titles, and so on, which are clearly contrary to the spirit of the Gospel. With titles come honours. And honours place us in danger of believing that we are more than we are, and cause us to forget that we are supposed to be servants.

REFLECTION — *Looking into the mirror*

Christ's harshest words were directed, not at sinners, but at religious people such as the Scribes and Pharisees. What were the main faults he found in them?

They didn't practise what they preached. They made things impossible for ordinary people by multiplying rules, and demanding exact observance of those rules, without offering the slightest help to those who found them burdensome. They sought their own honour, rather than the honour of God. And the most damning thing of all – they lacked charity and compassion in their dealings with others.

The Scribes and Pharisees were not unique. They could be any group of religious people any time and anywhere. The picture Christ painted of them was not a flattering one. But it is a mirror into which we too are invited to look. If we do look into this mirror, we will see our own face there, for we have some if not all of their faults.

Which of us can truthfully say that our deeds match our words?

Do we not sometimes consider ourselves better than others? Do we not lay down the law for others while excusing ourselves? Do we not demand sacrifices of others which we don't demand of ourselves? Do we not like to be noticed, and to take the best seat – if we can get it? Are we too not lacking in charity, compassion, and a spirit of service?

The real tragedy of the Scribes and Pharisees wasn't the fact that they had faults, but that they were blind to those faults. Yet many of them were sincere and pious people. But what good is piety if it doesn't make us more humble, more loving, and more compassionate? Piety is no substitute for goodness.

REFLECTION — *Make yourselves clean*

The First Reading is a call to repentance addressed to the rulers of Sodom and Gomorrah, two cities synonymous with evil. The prophet Isaiah said to them, 'Wash, make yourselves clean.' He promised that the Lord would grant them complete pardon if they heeded the call to repentance. If they didn't, disaster awaited them. This was not meant as a threat. What comes across here is God's concern for the inhabitants of the two cities.

Now when the prophet said, 'Wash, make yourselves clean', he wasn't talking about a purely exterior ritual washing as laid down by the Law. He was talking about an interior cleansing of the heart.

In the Gospel Jesus directs some harsh words at the Scribes and Pharisees. One of the hardest things he said about them was: 'Alas for you, Scribes and Pharisees. You hypocrites! You clean the outside of cup and dish and leave the inside full of corruption. Clean the inside of cup and dish and the outside will become clean as well.'

The problem with the Pharisees was that they saw evil as something entirely outside themselves. But Jesus said that the source of evil is within us. It has its roots in the heart. Corruption of heart is the worst kind of badness – it is to be bad at the core.

'Wash, make yourselves clean.' This same message is delivered to us during Lent. We must not be content with exterior cleanness. We must seek cleanness of heart. We must purify the source. The heart is the source. It is the well-spring from which our thoughts, desires, words, and deeds flow. If the heart is clean, then all that flows from it will be clean, like water flowing from an unpolluted spring.

How does one purify the heart? By focusing on love. That's why the prophet goes on the say: 'Cease to do evil. Learn to do good.' Love purifies the heart. The heart is holy ground. On this holy ground we will see and meet God.

REFLECTION — *God's mercy towards repentant sinners*

Once there was a man who committed a terrible crime. It was so terrible that he thought there could be no forgiveness for him. In fact, he felt he was already damned even before he died. He tried to forget about the foul deed, but the more he tried to forget it, the more it haunted him.

One day he was passing a church where a mission was in progress. Before he knew it, he found himself inside. He sneaked into a seat at the back. He was feeling so ashamed of himself that he didn't even look up. He imagined that everyone in church knew what he had done and had condemned him.

However, after a while he found himself listening to what the missioner was saying. He was talking about the greatness of God's mercy. He quoted the words we've just heard in the First Reading: 'Though your sins are like scarlet, they shall be as white as snow; though they are red as crimson, they shall become white as wool.' Then he went on to say, 'Even if someone had killed his own mother, God would forgive him if he repented.'

Afterwards the man went to talk to the priest. Trembling he

said, 'You know that man you were talking about in your sermon?'

'What man?' asked the priest.

'The man who killed his own mother.'

'Oh, that man. What about him?'

'I am that man.'

With that, the priest took him aside. He listened to his sad
story, and gave him absolution. The man went away feeling that
there was hope for him after all. There is no sin which is beyond
the scope of God's pardon. And once we have confessed our
sins, and received the Lord's forgiveness, we should forgive ourselves. 'God loves us most when we love ourselves least' (St Au-
gustine).

PRAYER OF THE FAITHFUL

Celebrant: God listens to the prayers of the humble. Let us
with humility bring our needs before him.

Response: Lord, graciously hear us.

Reader(s): For the leaders of the Church: that they may practise in their own lives what they preach to others. [Pause] Lord,
hear us.

For all who hold public office: that they may not seek their
own glory but to be of service to others. [Pause] Lord, hear us.

For those who have committed serious crimes: that they may
repent so that they may receive God's bountiful forgiveness.
[Pause] Lord, hear us.

For all gathered here: that the practice of our religion may
help us to grow in love and compassion. [Pause] Lord, hear us.

For our own special needs. [Longer pause] Lord, hear us.

Celebrant: Lord, grant that what we have said with our lips, we
may believe with our hearts, and practise with our lives. We make
this prayer through Christ our Lord.

PRAYER / REFLECTION

The Scribes and Pharisees were more concerned

with *appearing* good than with actually *being* good.
We don't have to put on an outward show,
or pretend to be what we are not.
All we have to do is try to be true to what we are –
God's precious sons and daughters.
Lord, help us to shun all falsity and pretence,
and to live a life of genuine goodness.
Then our deeds will flow from what we are,
as naturally as good fruit from a good tree.

WEDNESDAY OF SECOND WEEK OF LENT

INTRODUCTION AND CONFITEOR

In today's readings we have a reference to the suffering of
the just. Jesus is the supreme example of this. To follow his way
will inevitably involve suffering. But there are great rewards too.
Let us turn to God, asking pardon for our failures. and strength
in our weakness. [Pause]

Lord Jesus, you give us strength when we are weak. Lord, have
mercy.

You give us courage when we are afraid. Christ, have mercy.

You raise us up when we fall down. Lord, have mercy.

SCRIPTURE NOTE

The *First Reading* (Jer 18:18-20) is part of a prayer in which
Jeremiah calls to God's attention how his enemies are plotting
against him. The very people whose cause he pleaded before
God are now digging a pit for him. They listen to his every word
in the hope of using what he says against him. Jeremiah pleads
with God to take heed of what they are saying about him, and to
take up his cause against them. The plotting against Jeremiah
prepares us for the *Gospel* (Mt 20:17-28) in which we have Matthew's third prediction of Jesus' Passion.

After this prediction comes the request of the mother of James and John. Her request reflects popular belief about the glory that would belong to the Messiah. The fact that the request came immediately after the third prediction of the passion shows that neither she nor the apostles had taken on board the reality of the sufferings of the Messiah.

Jesus told the two apostles that the assignment of places in the kingdom belonged not to him but to the Father. But what they could have, provided they really wanted it, was to be closely associated with him in his suffering. (The implication is that if they shared his suffering, they would also share his glory).

When the request caused indignation among the other apostles, Jesus told them how authority should be exercised among them. They must not copy the Gentiles, among whom authority is exercised as power. Among them authority must be exercised as service. He set the example himself. He came 'not to be served but to serve, and to give his life as a ransom for many' (a reference to his saving death).

REFLECTION — *Leadership as service*

The mother of James and John asked Jesus if her sons could have the top two positions in his Kingdom. The boldness of her request is stunning. Obviously she thought that Jesus' kingdom would be modelled on worldly kingdoms. Those in high places would enjoy honour, glory, and power, and would lord it over their subjects.

But Jesus told her that it wouldn't be like that at all. In his kingdom the rulers would be servants. He set the example himself. As Lord and Master he could have lorded it over the apostles. But he didn't. He made himself their servant. Instead of going on a power trip, he went the way of self-emptying love.

Timothy Radcliffe tells how when he was a student at Oxford a priest from another province of the Order came to visit their community. When he arrived, a Dominican was sweeping the hall. Presuming he was a Brother, the visitor said, 'Brother, go and get me a cup of coffee.' After the coffee, the visitor asked him to take his bags to his room. Finally the visitor said, 'Now, Brother, I wish to meet the Father Prior.' To which the 'Brother' replied, 'I am the Prior'.

This is a good example of what Jesus was talking about when he said that in his community those in authority should be the servants of their brothers and sisters. This shows the spiritual revolution brought by Jesus. He wanted to build a community in which the members would be liberated from rivalry, competition, and the struggle for power.

Self-sacrifice ought to be part of an authentic Christian life. But it is an essential element of Christian leadership. Loving service should be the chief characteristic of the Christian leader. Love is made visible in service. And it is by serving that we grow in love.

REFLECTION — *A kingdom of love and service*

In the third temptation, the devil took Jesus to the top of a high mountain from where he showed him all the kingdoms of the world and their splendour. And he said, 'All these I will give you, if you fall at my feet and worship me.'

This was the temptation to set up a political kingdom, with all the trappings of power and glory. It was a temptation that would be repeated during his public ministry. We find an echo of it in today's Gospel. This is precisely the kind of kingdom the mother of James and John had in mind when she asked Jesus if her two sons could have the two top places in his kingdom.

Jesus did indeed speak about a kingdom. In fact, he declared that the whole purpose of his coming was to establish a kingdom on earth. But it would not be a political kingdom, but a spiritual kingdom. And it would not be his own kingdom, but the kingdom of God. This kingdom would not be modelled on worldly kingdoms, as the apostles thought. In worldly kingdoms the rulers lord it over their subjects, and those in high places enjoy honour, power, and glory. In the kingdom of God the greatest are those who serve.

The third temptation was the temptation to replace love with power. Power offers an easy substitute for the hard task of love. But Jesus refused the way of power. He had come, not to rule people, but to serve them.

And this is how he wanted it to be in his community. The leaders would be the servants of their brothers and sisters. Service of itself won't ennoble us unless we can do it with love. It has to be an expression of love.

If one wants to serve the way Jesus suggests, one has to be ready to drink the cup he drank – the cup of sacrifice and suffering. Those who are willing to share the cup of suffering with him, will also share his glory.

REFLECTION — *Drinking the cup*

The Jews looked on life as a cup which contained a mixture of sweet and bitter things. It's a powerful image. At times the cup of life can be full of bitterness. At other times it can be overflowing with sweetness. At still other times it can be empty.

James and John wanted places of honour in Jesus' kingdom. They obviously thought that his kingdom would be modelled on worldly kingdoms. Those in high places would enjoy honour, glory, and power. But they got it completely wrong. In Jesus' kingdom the greatest would be those who were willing to serve.

So Jesus said to them, 'Can you drink the cup that I am to drink?' What Jesus was really asking them was, 'Are you willing to go through the suffering that I am going to go through?' They two disciples immediately said they were. But the fact was, they didn't know what that cup would contain. Nor did they know their own weakness. Because when the time came, far from drinking the cup with him, they abandoned him.

We don't know in advance what the cup of life holds for us. We find that out as we go along. But we can be sure that it will contain some bitter things. Jesus, the innocent one, chose to drink a very bitter cup for love of us. But he didn't find it easy.

In fact, when the moment came for him to drink it, he asked his Father to take it away from him. Nevertheless, drink it he did.

Hence, if we find the cup of life particularly bitter, there is no need for us to pretend that it is sweet, or to think that we can drink it by our own strength. Let us not be afraid or ashamed to say, 'No, Lord, I can't drink it. I don't want to drink it. But if I have to, help me with it.'

To drink a cup made difficult by a life of sacrifice and service of others is to follow Jesus. But those who share the bitterness of his cross will also share the sweetness of his Easter victory.

PRAYER OF THE FAITHFUL

Celebrant: The Lord loves justice and right, and fills the earth with his love. Let us with confidence bring our needs before him.

Response: Lord, graciously hear us.

Reader(s): For the Pope and the Bishops: that they may be true servants of the servants of God. [Pause] Lord, hear us.

For temporal rulers: that they may exercise their authority in a gentle and just manner. [Pause] Lord, hear us.

For those whose cup right now is filled with bitterness. [Pause] Lord, hear us.

For all gathered here: that we may not be ashamed to acknowledge our weakness, or too proud to ask for help. [Pause] Lord, hear us.

For our own special needs. [Longer pause] Lord, hear us.

Celebrant: God of power and love, cleanse our hearts of greed and envy. Give us the courage to drink from your Son's cup on earth, so that we may share his glory in heaven. We ask this through the same Christ our Lord.

PRAYER

The kingdom of God is not modelled on earthly kingdoms. In earthly kingdoms the rulers lord it over their subjects, and those in high places enjoy honour, power, and glory.

In the kingdom of God the greatest are those who serve.
If we want to serve the way Jesus suggests,
we have to be ready to drink the cup he drank –
the cup of sacrifice and suffering.
But those who share the cup of his suffering
will also share the cup of his Easter victory.

THURSDAY OF SECOND WEEK OF LENT

INTRODUCTION AND CONFITEOR

Those who trust in God are truly blessed. This may not always be evident in this world, where the good suffer and the evil prosper.

But God is the strength of those who trust in him. As we gather to celebrate the Eucharist, let us ask God to increase our trust in him. [Pause]

Lord Jesus, you are our refuge in times of distress. Lord, have mercy.

You never disappoint those who hope in you. Christ, have mercy.

You give life to those who trust in you. Lord, have mercy.

SCRIPTURE NOTE

The *First Reading* (Jer 17:5-10, a bit of wisdom poetry) contrasts the fate of the wicked who put their trust in the things of this world with that of the just who put their trust in God. The former are compared to a barren desert shrub; the latter to a fruitful tree planted beside a flowing stream. The reading goes on to talk about the perversity of the human heart. The secret plots of the heart are hidden to men, but are transparent to God.

The parable of the rich man and the poor man (*Gospel*, Lk 16:19-31) was addressed to the Pharisees who were fond of money (v. 14). It contrasts the fate of a rich man who put his trust in riches with that of a poor man who put his trust in God. The rich man's sin consisted in his blind indifference to the plight of the poor man. He was a worldling who didn't look beyond the good things of this life.

It is a parable about the responsibility of wealth. Some of the harshest words in the Bible are directed at the uncaring rich. On the other hand, Jesus declared the poor blessed. The poor are the 'little ones' who have no one to trust in but God.

REFLECTION — *Living in opposite worlds*

Dives and Lazarus lived in different worlds. Dives was dressed in purple robes; Lazarus was dressed in rags. Dives ate splendidly every day; Lazarus didn't eat at all. Dives was healthy; Lazarus was covered with sores. Dives lived in a palace; Lazarus lived in the streets.

In fact, to say that they lived in different worlds is an understatement. They lived in opposite worlds. Dives lived in a garden; Lazarus lived in a desert. Dives was in an earthly paradise; Lazarus in an earthly hell.

And yet, though their respective worlds were as different as day and night, they lay side by side. But the rich man never once entered the world of the poor man. He was indifferent to him, and indifference is the worst thing of all. Had he entered the poor man's lonely world, he surely would have felt compassion for him, and been moved to help him.

We can be within arm's reach of someone, yet be living in a different world from that person. We'll never know the difference unless we leave our world and enter that of the other person. We will never understand it from the outside.

Jesus entered fully into our world of suffering and death. His example should give us the courage and generosity of heart to enter the world of those who are in pain or in need. Then, having experienced what life is like for them, we will surely be moved to do what we can to help them.

If Lent did nothing else for us but cause us to open our hearts to those who are less fortunate than ourselves, it will prove to be a time of great grace for us.

REFLECTION — *Poverty and riches*

Dives and Lazarus lived in different worlds. Dives was dressed in purple robes; Lazarus was dressed in rags. Dives ate splendidly every day; Lazarus didn't eat at all. Dives was healthy; Lazarus was covered with sores. Dives lived in a palace; Lazarus lived in the streets.

In fact, to say that they lived in different worlds is an understatement. They lived in opposite worlds. Dives lived in a garden; Lazarus lived in a desert. Dives was in an earthly paradise; Lazarus in an earthly hell.

Lazarus was about as poor as any man could be. Yet, in a sense, Dives was even poorer. How could that be? Lazarus was suffering from material poverty. Dives was suffering from poverty of heart. His heart was devoid of compassion and love. Even the street dogs had more compassion than he.

Dives was condemned, not because he was rich, but because he didn't show compassion to the poor man. Sin is not just about doing wrong. It is also about not doing good. One of the greatest evils in the world is indifference towards one's neighbour.

The rich are wounded by their riches, just as the poor are wounded by their poverty. Riches make a person self-preoccupied. They blind a person and harden the heart. That is the real tragedy.

The only riches that are worth having are the riches of the heart. Jesus compared the heart to a storehouse (Luke 6:45). If we wish to know how wealthy we are, let us not waste our time counting our possessions, or looking into our bank account. Let us look rather into the storehouse of our heart. A compassionate heart is great wealth.

REFLECTION — *A disturbing encounter*

Today we call people like Lazarus 'down-and-outs'. From time to time all of us encounter people like that. I think it is true to say that most of us find such encounters disturbing and humbling experiences. Why is this?

They are disturbing because they arouse within us conflicting feelings of pity, discomfort, anger, and guilt. They are humbling because they make us realise that we too are poor, only in a different way. Down-and-outs are poor materially. We are poor in compassion, poor in our willingness to help, poor in our capacity to love. In other words, poor at heart.

But such encounters can also be a blessing. They can act as a reminder to us that before God all of us are poor. They can awaken within us feelings of tenderness and compassion. Thus they can bring our heart to life, and enable us to enter the world of the poor and the excluded.

The only riches that are worth having are the riches of the heart. Jesus compared the heart to a storehouse (Luke 6:45). If we wish to know how wealthy we are, let us not waste our time counting our possessions or looking into our bank account. Let us look rather into the storehouse of our heart. A generous heart is great wealth.

However, at the end of the day only God sees what is in the heart, and only God can make the heart what it is meant to be.

REFLECTION — *The cry of the poor*

A man went out on Monday. It was a cold winter's day. At a street corner he came upon a ragged little girl begging. He was so shocked at her condition that her image haunted him for the rest of the day. That night he slept very little.

He went out on Tuesday. She was there again, in the same spot, with the same sad expression on her small, weather-beaten face. His heart bled with pity for her. He didn't get much sleep that night either.

He went out on Wednesday. He approached the location with dread. Yes, she was there again. He felt shame and guilt for her sad condition, and said to himself, 'I must do something for her.' But he quickly added, 'Not today; I'm too busy today.' That night the little girl again robbed him of some sleep.

He went out on Thursday. On seeing the girl he got angry and exclaimed, 'It's a disgrace! Why doesn't somebody help her? Where are her parents?' He slept somewhat better that night.

He went out on Friday. Unable to bear the thought of seeing the little girl, he crossed to the other side of the street. However, he saw her in his mind's eye, and that was just as bad. That night he fell asleep as soon as he hit the pillow. But the little girl visited him in his dreams.

He went out on Saturday. He was late and was rushing. Before he knew it, he had passed the street corner where the girl was. Suddenly he realised, that not only had he not looked at the child, but he hadn't thought of her either. Nor did he think much about her for the rest of the day. That night he slept soundly.

On Sunday he didn't go out at all, except to go to church.

PRAYER OF THE FAITHFUL

*Celebrant:*God is the strength of those who trust in him. Let our prayers today be an expression of our trust in God and our concern for others.

Response: Lord, hear our prayer.

Reader(s): For Christians: that they may not be indifferent to the needs of those around them. [Pause] Let us pray to the Lord.

For government leaders: that they may be tireless in their efforts to eliminate poverty. [Pause] Let us pray to the Lord.

For those who through unemployment, poverty, or sickness sit on the sidelines of life. [Pause] Let us pray to the Lord.

For all in this congregation: that we may strive to make ourselves rich in compassion rather than in the things of this world. [Pause] Let us pray to the Lord.

For our own special needs. [Longer pause] Let us pray to the Lord

Celebrant: God of love and mercy, fill our hearts with your love.

Give us the grace to rise above our selfishness, and keep us faithful to you and to one another. We ask this through Christ our Lord.

PRAYER / REFLECTION

Those who trust in God are truly blessed;
God himself becomes their strength.
They are like a tree planted by the waterside.
It has no worries in time of drought;
its foliage stays green,
and it never ceases to bear fruit.
Lord, give us the kind of trust in you
that will sustain us in times of difficulty,
that will make our lives fruitful,
and that will keep our hope unfading.

FRIDAY OF SECOND WEEK OF LENT

INTRODUCTION AND CONFITEOR

God cared for his people like a good gardener cares for his vineyard. But they failed to produce the fruits of justice, love, and peace.

We are the new people of God. God looks to us to produce the fruits of Christian living. Sadly, we often fail. Let us call to mind our sins, especially those of omission. [Pause]

I confess to almighty God ...

SCRIPTURE NOTE

The *First Reading* (Gen 37:3-4.12-13.18-20) contains the story of the betrayal of Joseph by his brothers. The cause of the brothers' hatred is Jacob's preferential love for Joseph, the son of his old age. This love was expressed in the gift of a special tunic. What happened to Joseph foreshadows what will happen to Jesus, the Father's beloved Son. This is the connection with the

Gospel (Mt 21:33-43.45-46).

The parable of the wicked vine dressers tells of God's goodness to his people, and of their failure to respond in kind. It was addressed to the chief priests and elders, and was meant as a warning.

The parable is an allegory of God's dealings with his people. The landowner is God. The vineyard is Israel. The wicked tenants are the people of Israel, but more especially the religious leaders, who had been given charge of the vineyard by God. The servants are the prophets, sent by God and so often rejected and killed. The son is Jesus himself.

Sadly, the warning went unheeded. Jerusalem was destroyed, and the Gentiles replaced the Jews as God's people. All this would have been clear to Matthew's readers because it had already happened.

REFLECTION — Producing the fruits

The people of Israel had been treated in a privileged manner by God. He had bestowed on them the sort of love and care that a dedicated vine dresser bestows on a vineyard. But privilege brings responsibility. They were meant to produce the fruits of right living. Sadly, they failed.

God looked for peace from his people, and got war; for true worship, and got idolatry; for justice in their dealings with one another, and got injustice, corruption, and exploitation of the poor and the weak; for goodness, and got evil; for caring and sharing, and got greed and acquisitiveness; for temperance, and got excessive eating and drinking; for community, and got exclusiveness and snobbery; for humility, and got pride; for wise and godly living, and got a pagan lifestyle.

Yet God didn't give up on them. He sent messenger after messenger to them (the prophets). But far from listening to them, they abused some of them and killed others. God was disappointed in them, not for his own sake, but for their sake. They squandered the blessings he wanted them to enjoy. Sadly, the vineyard was destined to become a wilderness.

This to some extent is our story too. God wants us to make use of the gifts and opportunities he has given us so that we can grow as his children. But often we fail to respond to his love. And yet God doesn't write us off, but gives us chance after chance.

We fail not just as individuals but as Church. The Christian community is the vineyard Christ planted and for which he gave his life. He looks to us, the tenants of his vineyard, to produce the fruits of justice, love, and peace. It's a great privilege but a great challenge too.

REFLECTION — *Overcoming evil with good*

What was done to Joseph by his brothers was evil. He was an innocent youth, and did not deserve to be treated like that. He bore them no ill-will. The father was partly to blame because he showed favouritism to Joseph, thus arousing envy in his brothers, an envy that quickly turned into hatred.

It shows how dangerous it is to allow thoughts of hatred to take hold in our minds. Evil nurtured quickly grows.

Reuben, however, refused to go along with the decision of the others. He was faithful to his own conscience, ultimately saving his brother's life. The integrity of one person can transform a bad situation.

Joseph ended up a slave in Egypt. There he eventually rose to be prime minister. He achieved this, not by cunning, but by virtue – by sheer goodness, tenacity, and talent. When a famine came, and the brothers came to Egypt looking for food, Joseph could have taken revenge on them. But he refused to return evil or evil. Instead, he forgive his brothers and saved their lives.

The story of Joseph is one of the greatest stories in the Bible. What makes it so great is the fact that in it good triumphs over evil, love triumphs over hatred. Joseph is a model for all those who suffer unjustly in the cause of right. In all the events of his life the hand of God was with him. It was faith in God that enabled him to endure all his sufferings and emerge triumphant.

The story of Joseph prepares us for the story of Jesus, the Father's beloved Son, sold by one of his friends, who became the saviour of all. Here again we see good coming out of evil.

Both stories show us that there is only one way to overcome evil, and that is with good.

REFLECTION — *The danger of envy*

It is said that favourites have no friends. 'Joseph's brothers seeing how his father loved him more than all his other sons, came to hate him so much that they could not say a civil word to him.'

Even though the brothers carry most of the blame for what happened to Joseph, the father is not blameless either. By showing favouritism to Joseph, he aroused envy in his other sons, an envy that quickly turned into hatred.

Envy is defined as 'a feeling of grudging aroused by the possessions, achievements, or qualities of another person.' The other person has something we don't have, but which we would like to have. The brothers saw that Joseph enjoyed his father's love. They begrudged him this, and hated him because of it.

All of us are subject to envy. Envy is not something to be ashamed of. We see others as having things we don't have – possessions, or talents, or achievements. Naturally we are envious of them. However, if allowed to run its natural course, envy can be very dangerous. It can destroy relationships and cause great unhappiness.

When we are envious of people we see them as greater than we are. Their greatness makes us feel small. Therefore we are tempted to cut them down to size. Without going as far as Joseph's brothers went, we can still be very hurtful towards them. We may criticise them, refuse to work with them, refuse them friendship or even simple courtesy. We may even come to hate them. One thing is sure, we won't love them.

Envy stems from a longing for goodness and wholeness. It can point us in the right direction. It can spur us to imitate the virtues of others. Above all, it should cause us to recognise and be grateful for the gifts God has given us, and spur us to make good use of them. Gratitude drives out envy.

PRAYER OF THE FAITHFUL

Celebrant: God did not spare his own Son but gave him up to death on our behalf. Therefore, let us bring our needs before him with great confidence.

Response: Lord, graciously hear us.

Reader(s): For the Christian community, the vineyard of Christ: that it may produce the fruits of justice, love and peace. [Pause] Lord, hear us.

For civil leaders: that they may be responsible in carrying out their duties. [Pause] Lord, hear us.

For families that are experiencing brokenness and division. [Pause] Lord, hear us.

For those who have been the victims of unjust and hurtful treatment. [Pause] Lord, hear us.

For grace to be willing to forgive those who have sinned against us, and never to return evil for evil. [Pause] Lord, hear us.

For our own special needs. [Longer pause] Lord, hear us.

Celebrant: Lord, in your unfailing compassion, watch over your Church. Turn us away evil, and direct us into the way of good. We make this prayer through Christ our Lord.

PRAYER / REFLECTION

Jesus says to us what he said to his apostles:
'I am the vine, you are the branches.
United with me, you will bear much fruit.
Separated from me, you can do nothing.'
The fruit which Jesus desires from us is primarily that of love.
Lord, with your patient urging,
help us to produce the fruits of love,
and thus the world know
that we are living branches of you, the True Vine.

SATURDAY OF SECOND WEEK OF LENT

INTRODUCTION AND CONFITEOR

'Father I have sinned against heaven and before you.' So said the prodigal son whose story we hear in today's Gospel. As we call to mind our sins, we might make our own the words and sentiments of the prodigal son. [Pause] Fortunately for us God is prodigal with his forgiveness.

Lord Jesus, you are kind and full of compassion. Lord, have mercy.

You are slow to anger and abounding in love. Christ, have mercy.

You do not treat us according to our sins, nor repay us according to our faults. Lord, have mercy.

SCRIPTURE NOTE

The theme of both readings is that of God's mercy towards sinners. The *First Reading* (Mic 7:14-15.18-20) is a prayer in which Micah addresses God as the shepherd of his people. The prophet asks God to bring his flock out of the forest and into fertile pastures. He appeals to the Lord to work signs comparable to those of the Exodus. Unlike false gods, the God of Israel is a God who 'delights in showing mercy'. Hence, the prophet confidently appeals to him to pardon the sins of his people, and not to renage on the covenant he made with their fathers long ago.

The fact that Jesus welcomed sinners and ate with them was a cause of scandal to the Pharisees (*Gospel*, Lk 15:1-3, 11-32). They, the 'separated ones', avoided all contact with sinners. They assumed that God had no dealings with sinners either. But Jesus showed them a very different kind of God. In the parable of the Prodigal Son he illustrates what the First Reading said, namely, that God delights in showing mercy to repentant sinners.

REFLECTION   Lessons of the story

Some people believe that the story of the prodigal son is an unfair story. They maintain that the older son got a raw deal, and that the younger son got away with murder.

The first thing that needs to be said is that the younger son behaved very badly. He betrayed his family, himself, and the whole Jewish way of life. But he redeemed himself by coming back home and asking for forgiveness. It's easy to come back home when one is a hero, laden with trophies. But he came home laden with shame and disgrace. He deserved to be punished, and even asked for it. Yet punishment was the last thing he needed. In any case, he had already been punished; the experience had turned out to be a horrible one.

As for the older son, he cut a sad figure. He couldn't find in his heart the generosity to reach out a welcoming hand to his brother. Instead, he grew resentful, and so was unable to share his father's joy. Joy and resentment cannot co-exist in the same heart.

The story was aimed at the Pharisees who were critical of Jesus because of the sympathetic attitude he adopted towards sinners. Essentially Jesus was telling them three things.

The first concerned God: God is never happier than when welcoming back repentant sinners.

The second concerned himself: he had been sent to bring home the lost children of God.

The third concerned themselves: the older son was a mirror image of them. The problem with the older son was that he didn't see himself as a sinner. That was their problem too. If they saw themselves as sinners, they would have a more compassionate attitude towards sinners.

The story doesn't give us a licence to sin. But it does show that if, through human weakness or wickedness, we do sin, then we can come back. We can make a fresh start. As soon as we repent and throw ourselves on the mercy of God, we are restored to our inheritance and clothed in the 'garment' of salvation.

REFLECTION — *Loved in our sins*

The decision to come home was not an easy one for the prodigal. It's easy to come back home when you are a hero, laden with trophies. But he was coming home empty-handed. He was a failure. Worse – he was a sinner. He was coming home laden with shame and disgrace. He deserved to be punished, and even asked for it.

What happened? When the father saw his lost son coming towards him, his heart went out to him, and next minute they were in each other's arms.

The father didn't merely receive his son back; he welcomed him back. That welcome was no half-hearted or grudging affair. It was warm, whole-hearted, and prodigally generous.

This love is available also to us. In and through our sins we experience the love and mercy of God. God doesn't just forgive us; God loves us, and lets us know it. It doesn't do us much good to be loved for being perfect. We need to be accepted and loved precisely as sinners.

It is an extraordinary experience to be loved in one's sinfulness. Only the person who has experienced this kind of love can know what it is. Being loved like this puts us in touch with our true nature, and to touch our true nature is to come home.

The parable doesn't give us a licence to sin. But it does show that if, through human weakness or wickedness, we do sin, then we can come back. We can make a fresh start. This is the great lesson of the parable.

The story also shows us what repentance means. To repent is to turn one's life around. It is to turn back to God, and to walk in his love. The only thing that truly heals people is unconditional love.

REFLECTION — *What the heart of God is like*

Jesus scandalised the Pharisees by the sympathetic attitude he adopted towards sinners. He didn't wait for sinners to come to him; he sought them out. In associating with sinners he wasn't condoning their situation. Rather, he was trying to show them a better way.

But what really scandalised the Pharisees was the fact that Jesus did not wait for sinners to repent before befriending them. He befriended them *while they were still sinners.* The Pharisees would have nothing to do with sinners. They assumed that God had nothing to do with them either. The central dogma of their religion was: 'God loves the virtuous, and hates the sinner.' But in the parable of the prodigal son Jesus showed them a very different kind of God.

In his attitude towards sinners, Jesus shows us what the heart of God is like. What made the God of Israel different from false gods was his capacity to show mercy to sinners. In the words of the prophet Micah (First Reading), he is a God 'who delights in showing mercy'. Not only does God forgive the sins of his people, but he delights in doing so.

As religious people, the Pharisees ought to have known what God was like. But they didn't. Since they had no sense of being sinners themselves, they had no compassion for sinners. They were like the older son in the story. True, he was a dutiful son. However, in spite of his fidelity to duty, he was unable to show compassion to his younger brother. Of what use is religion if it doesn't make us more compassionate towards those who fall?

It is easy to adopt the attitude of the older son. When we do that, a coldness grows inside me. We may be doing all the right things, but we have no joy or love in our hearts, All we have is anger, resentment, and self-righteousness. That is not a good place to be.

PRAYER OF THE FAITHFUL

Celebrant: The father in Jesus' story is God the Father. Therefore, let us turn to him with confidence and place our needs before him.

Response: Lord, hear our prayer.

Reader(s): For the Church: that through its ministry sinners may experience the love and mercy of God. [Pause] Let us pray to the Lord.

For parents: that they may create homes where their children will know they are loved. [Pause)] Let us pray to the Lord.

For those who have strayed, and who haven't yet returned to the Father's house. [Pause] Let us pray to the Lord.

For all gathered here: that, having experienced the goodness of God in our own regard, we may show kindness and compassion to others. [Pause] Let us pray to the Lord.

For our own special needs. [Longer pause] Let us pray to the Lord.

Celebrant: Lord God, you reveal you power most of all in your forgiveness and compassion. Fill us with your grace so that we may walk with joy in the way of your commandments. We make this prayer through Christ our Lord.

REFLECTION

The prodigal son had no trophies to show his father.
He was a failure. Worse – he was a sinner.
He deserved to be punished.
Yet punishment was the last thing he needed.
When the father saw his lost son coming towards him,
his heart went out to him,
and next minute they were in each other's arms.
It is an extraordinary experience to be loved in one's sins.
Those who have experienced this kind of love,
know something about the heart of God.

Third Week of Lent

MONDAY OF THIRD WEEK OF LENT

INTRODUCTION AND CONFITEOR

Jesus came, not to condemn the world, but to save the world.

Nevertheless, like so many prophets, Jesus was rejected by his own people. We too may reject him by not allowing him into our lives. [Pause]

Lord Jesus, you were sent to bring the good news of salvation to the poor. Lord, have mercy.

You were sent to bind up hearts that are broken. Christ, have mercy.

You were sent to give sight to the blind and to set the downtrodden free. Lord, have mercy.

SCRIPTURE NOTE

The *First Reading* (2 Kgs 5:1-15) tells the story of the cure and conversion of Naaman. Naaman was commander of the Syrian army, and therefore a Gentile. His cure is referred to in the Gospel, where his faith is contrasted with the lack of faith of the people of Nazareth.

To understand today's *Gospel* (Lk 4:24-30) we need to see it in its context. In the course of his sermon in the synagogue at Nazareth Jesus had declared that Isaiah's messianic vision of pardon, healing, and liberation (61:1-2) was about to become a reality. The people greeted the news with enthusiasm. But when he claimed a central role for himself in bringing this about, their enthusiasm turned into scepticism.

They still saw him as just the son of Joseph, a local carpenter. How could such a one as he fulfil the messianic vision? And yet they had heard that he had done great things in Capernaum. They wondered why he hadn't done them among them. His answer was that it was due to their lack of faith. This didn't go down well with them. (Today's Gospel tells us what happened next).

He went on to hint at the inclusion of the Gentiles in the messianic blessings, giving two examples of Gentiles who had been helped by two of their greatest prophets, Elijah and Elisha. At this point things turned ugly. How dare he suggest that Gentiles would be put on the same footing as Jews!

The Jews had forgotten that they were called to be 'a light to the nations'. It was this exclusivism that led to the trouble in the synagogue. Jesus challenged this. However, instead of looking at themselves, they turned on him, and tried to kill him. But he escaped through their midst. This incident foreshadows the ultimate fate of Jesus.

REFLECTION — *Bringing out the best or the worst*

In the synagogue at Nazareth Jesus declared that the messianic vision of pardon, healing, and liberation was about to become a reality. The people greeted the news with enthusiasm. But when he claimed a central role for himself in bringing this about, their enthusiasm turned into scepticism.

They still saw him as just the son of Joseph, a local carpenter. How could such a one as he fulfil the messianic vision? And yet they had heard that he had done great things in Capernaum. They wondered why he hadn't done them among them.

He told them that it was because of their lack of faith. This didn't go down well with them. But then he went on to hint at the inclusion of the Gentiles in the messianic blessings, giving two examples of Gentiles who had been helped by two of their greatest prophets, Elijah and Elisha. It was at this point that things turned ugly. As Jews, they despised Gentiles. So, in a burst of nationalistic fervour, they turned on him, and tried to kill him. But he escaped through their midst.

It is a shocking incident. What makes it so shocking is the fact that it was done in the name of religion. Religion is a beautiful thing, but it can get distorted and turn into something repulsive. Religion then becomes synonymous with intolerance, fanaticism, and bigotry.

Religion brings out the worst in some people. It makes them more bigoted, and more apt to hate and kill. But religion brings out the best in other people. It makes them more tolerant and more loving. True religion fosters harmonious relationships with others. Religion is beautiful when it is like this.

There is an essential link between faith and love. We can't worship God if our heart is full of bitterness and hatred. Hatred towards any human being and love of God cannot exist in the same heart.

REFLECTION — *A blessing in disguise*

Naaman had a prestigious job – commander of the Syrian army. He had all the trappings of worldly success – wealth, power, fame. He felt no need of God. Therefore, religion played no part in his life.

Yet there seems to have been a basic goodness and decency about him. He was brave, honest, generous, and reliable. But then he contracted leprosy, and suddenly his world began to collapse.

Desperate for a cure, he swallowed his pride and sought help from the prophet Elisha in Israel, the little country he had plundered. However, what he was looking for was a 'quick fix' so that he could go back and resume his old life exactly as before.

But he discovered that there was no 'quick fix'. He had to be humble and patient. He had to learn to take orders for a change. But it proved well worth it because, not only was he cured of his leprosy, but he was converted as well.

On being cured of leprosy, he returned to Elisha and acknowledged Yahweh as the supreme and only God. So in the end he had reason to give thanks for his leprosy, because through it he received the gift of faith.

We are not unlike Naaman. In good times we forget God, even though we may continue to pay lip-service to him. But then an illness, or alcoholism, or some such thing, brings us to our knees, and we come face to face with our poverty, weakness, and mortality. We realise how flimsy are the foundations on which we have built our hopes. However, if this brings us closer to God, and makes us more spiritual, it will prove to be a blessing in disguise.

Some converts are 'Good Friday' converts – they enter the

Kingdom through the gates of suffering.

REFLECTION — *Rejected by his own*

Jesus went back to Nazareth and to the people among whom he had grown up. He wanted to bring them too the benefit of his gifts. They were the people who knew him best. You would have thought, then, that they would have appreciated him most. Sadly, they had no faith in him.

A person is never a hero to his own relations. A genius is not likely to be discovered by his friends. The person near at hand suffers because his faults and limitations are clearly visible. The person far away, on the other hand, is held in esteem because only his virtues are visible.

But what happened to Jesus at Nazareth went deeper than this. It wasn't just that they did not appreciate him. They rejected him. Why? Because he pointed out their lack of faith, and told them that the messianic promises were meant, not just for Jews, but for Gentiles too.

Jesus shared the fate of every true prophet – rejection by his own people. It's very hurtful to be rejected by one's own. Jesus was saddened by what happened to him at Nazareth, but he didn't get embittered and bury his gifts. He did what he could for the few who believed in him, and then took his gifts elsewhere.

Often we fail to appreciate the gifts and talents of those who are close to us. We don't recognise them, we don't give them a chance, we put them down.

If we ourselves have suffered the fate of not being appreciated by our own, we must not become embittered. We must let our light shine in spite of all.

PRAYER OF THE FAITHFUL

Celebrant: With gratitude in our hearts for all God's past benefits to us, let us bring our present needs before him now.

Response: Lord, graciously hear us.

Reader(s): For all believers: that their faith may be reflected in their lives. [Pause] Lord, hear us.

For the prophetical people in our world: that they may have the courage to persevere. [Pause] Lord, hear us.

For the sick and those who minister to them. [Pause] Lord, hear us.

For all in this congregation: that the practice of our religion may make us more tolerant and loving towards others. [Pause[Lord, hear us.

For our own special needs. [Longer pause] Lord, hear us.

Celebrant: Lord, send your Spirit to make us strong in faith and active in good works; alone and unaided we cannot please you. We make this prayer through Christ our Lord.

REFLECTION

Religion brings out the worst in some people,
making them more bigoted and more apt to hate.
Religion is repulsive when it is like this.
But religion brings out the best in other people,
making them more tolerant and more loving.
Religion is beautiful when it is like this.
There is an essential link between faith and love.
Hatred towards any human being and love of God
cannot exist in the same heart.

TUESDAY OF THIRD WEEK OF LENT

INTRODUCTION AND CONFITEOR

We always begin Mass by asking forgiveness for our sins. As we do so, we should also ask for the grace to forgive those who have sinned against us. [Pause]

Lord Jesus, a humble and contrite heart you will not spurn. Lord, have mercy.

You treat us gently, as you yourself are gentle and very merciful. Christ, have mercy.

You will not allow those who trust in you to be disappointed. Lord, have mercy.

SCRIPTURE NOTE

The Babylonian exile was the lowest point in the history of God's people. During that exile three young Israelites (Shadrach, Meshach and Abednego) were thrown into a fiery furnace by king Nebuchadnezzar because they refused to worship an idol.

The *First Reading* (Dan 3:25; 34-43) is part of the prayer made by one of them, Azariah (Abednego), from the furnace. In it he appeals, not only for their own salvation, but for the salvation of his people. He appeals to God to remember the covenant he made with Abraham, Isaac and Jacob. Without a leader or a prophet or a place of worship, the only thing they have to offer God is a contrite soul and a humble spirit. He prays that in future they may follow God whole-heartedly.

Azariah and his companions were in a desperate situation. The *Gospel* (Mt 18:21-35) tells of another man who was in a desperate situation. He owed his king a very large sum of money with the result that the king ordered that he and his entire family be sold as slaves. All he could do was beg for mercy. This he did very humbly. The king took pity on him and wrote off the debt. But he then couldn't do the same for a fellow servant who owed him a small sum of money.

The debt the servant owed was so large as to be beyond repayment. This is the strong point of the parable. This is our situation as sinners before God. We can't earn God's forgiveness; all we can do is ask for it. The message of the parable is clear: We must be willing to extend to others the generous forgiveness God has extended to us. Anyone who is forgiven has an obligation to forgive.

REFLECTION — *Healing the wounded heart*

There is no point in being glib about forgiveness. Forgiveness is never easy. The memory of wrongs done to us seeps into our heart, producing a legacy of bitterness. This is what makes forgiveness so hard but also so necessary. It is precisely the heart that is wounded. Unless we forgive, the heart can't heal.

To forgive is, first and foremost, a duty we owe ourselves. We forgive for the sake of our own well-being. We forgive because we don't want to live with feelings of resentment and desire for revenge. We forgive in order to cleanse ourselves of these poisonous attitudes and states of mind, so that we may be able to devote all our energies to loving, which is the only activity that befits a Christian.

One of the things that can motivate us to forgive is an appreciation of our own need of forgiveness. Jesus says that unless we forgive others God won't forgive us. The fault is not with God but with us. When we refuse to forgive we break down the bridge over which we ourselves must pass.

When we forgive, we ourselves are the main beneficiaries. But forgiveness also benefits the person who is forgiven. It sets the person free to walk in friendship with God and with the person he/she has offended.

We constantly fall short of complete forgiveness. Perhaps this is why Jesus tells us that we have to forgive seventy times seven. There is no moment when one is not in need of forgiveness nor any moment when one does not need to be forgiving.

Forgiveness doesn't mean forgetting the wrong done to us. It means remembering and letting go. Forgiveness is one of the highest and most beautiful forms of love. It is a holy task. Only God can help us to accomplish it fully.

REFLECTION — *Forgiveness*

The servant in Jesus' story owed the king so much money that even if he worked forever, he would not be able to repay him. His position was absolutely hopeless. All he could do was beg for mercy.

His situation was similar to that of Azariah. Acknowledging

his sins (and those of his people), Azariah cried out to God for deliverance from the midst of the furnace. There was nothing he could do to win deliverance. All he could do was throw himself on the mercy of God.

This is our situation before God. We can't win God's forgiveness. Sin against God cannot be wiped out by us. So what can we do?

1. We can humbly acknowledge our sins before God.
2. We can plead for God's mercy.
3. We can show a willingness to forgive those who sin against us.

Of the three, the third is the most difficult. It is also the most necessary, because without it we will not be forgiven. The problem does not lie with God; it lies with us. When we refuse to forgive others we make it impossible for ourselves to receive God's forgiveness. It is like two people living in the same room, one of whom closes the blind because he doesn't want the other to enjoy the sunlight. But in so doing he also deprives himself of the sunlight.

We need to pray for the gift of forgiveness. Unless we forgive we will not be able to let go of bitterness and resentment, and so will not know peace or healing.

We have to make a decision to forgive. But this doesn't mean that feelings of hurt and bitterness will suddenly disappear. The healing of these will take time. Forgiveness doesn't mean forgetting the wrong done to us. It means remembering and letting go.

Jesus says: 'You must forgive your brother *from your heart.*' It is only with the heart that we can forgive rightly. If forgiveness is to be effective it must be sincere and warm. A cold forgiveness is not much use.

REFLECTION — *The process of forgiveness*

Jesus asks us to forgive, not just once or twice, but always. Forgiveness is never easy. Without the grace of God it is sometimes impossible. When we get hurt, we grow resentful and bitter. Resentment and bitterness are very damaging things, and we cannot be healed of them unless we forgive.

We all need to forgive because at one time or another we all have been hurt. What can we do? We have to remember that forgiveness is *a process*. It cannot be achieved overnight. There are steps we can take that will lead to forgiveness and healing of the hurt.

1. We must recognise that we have suffered a hurt.
2. We must recognise that we have feelings about this. We feel angry and hurt. These feelings are not sins. They are natural and even healthy.
3. We should share our feelings about what has been done to us with someone we trust.
4. We should make a decision about our relationship with the person who has hurt us – whether to continue it or discontinue it. Forgiveness doesn't always lead to reconciliation because it takes two to be reconciled.
5. We should make a decision to forgive. Forgiveness is an act of the will, not of the feelings. But this doesn't mean that feelings of hurt and bitterness will suddenly disappear. The healing of these will take time. Forgiveness doesn't mean forgetting the wrong done to us. It means remembering and letting go.

One of the things that can motivate us to forgive is an appreciation of our own need of forgiveness. Forgiveness is one of the highest and most beautiful forms of love. It is a holy task. Only God can help us to accomplish it fully.

PRAYER OF THE FAITHFUL

Celebrant: Let us now turn in prayer to the God who forgives all our guilt and crowns us with love and compassion.

Response: Lord, hear our prayer.

Reader(s): For Christians: that they may give an example of forgiveness to the world. [Pause] Let us pray to the Lord.

For those who have been badly sinned against, and who are unable to forgive. [Pause] Let us pray to the Lord.

For grace to forgive those who have sinned against us, and so be healed of resentment and bitterness. [Pause] Let us pray to the Lord.

For the humility and courage to seek forgiveness of those we have offended. [Pause] Let us pray to the Lord.

For our own special needs. [Longer pause] Let us pray to the Lord.

Celebrant: All-powerful God, grant that we who stand always in need of your mercy, may be ready to show mercy to others. We ask this through Christ our Lord.

PRAYER

A prayer found in Auschwitz:
'Lord, remember not only people of good will,
but also people of ill will.
Do not remember only the sufferings
that have been inflicted on us,
but remember too the fruit we have bought
as a result of this suffering:
the comradeship and loyalty, the humility and courage,
the generosity and greatness of heart that has grown out of it.
And when they come to judgment,
let all the fruits that we have borne be their forgiveness.'

WEDNESDAY OF THIRD WEEK OF LENT

INTRODUCTION AND CONFITEOR

God has given us laws, not to curtail our freedom, but to help us to use it wisely. But we sometimes kick against God's laws, and thus bring a lot of trouble on ourselves. Let us call to mind our sins, and ask God for forgiveness. [Pause]

Lord Jesus, you show the path to those who stray. Lord, have mercy.

You smooth the way for the upright. Christ, have mercy.

You guard the ways of the just. Lord, have mercy.

SCRIPTURE NOTE

The common theme of the readings is the Law of God. In the *First Reading* (Deut 4:1.5-9) Moses urges the people to be faithful to God's Law, without adding to it or subtracting from it (v.2). (They did add to the Law of God. They added their own traditions which came to be regarded as equally binding, and sometimes got in the way of God's Law).

God's Law is not a burden to be endured, but a source of life and wisdom. If they live by that Law, they will demonstrate their wisdom to all peoples, and people will be drawn to the true God.

In the *Gospel* (Mt 5:17-19) Jesus declares that he came, not to abolish the Law of Moses, but to fulfil it. He had several clashes with the Scribes and Pharisees over the Law. They were concerned with fulfilling the letter of the law; he was more concerned with fulfilling the spirit of the Law. And he distinguished between the Law of God (given through Moses) and the traditions that had been added to it. He didn't hesitate to set the latter aside when he found that they were defeating the purpose of God's Law.

For his own disciples he proposed new standards of goodness that transcend the Law of Moses. Christians live, not by the law of Moses, but by the law of Jesus.

REFLECTION — *Jesus and the Law*

The common theme of today's readings is the Law of God. Jesus himself was subject to law, both human and divine. Here we are concerned with Jesus' attitude to the Law of God. He found no fault with the law itself. His problem lay in the way it was interpreted and applied by the religious leaders.

For the Scribes and Pharisees it was *the letter* of the law that mattered. For Jesus it was *the spirit* of the law that mattered. The important thing is not how many commandments we obey, but the spirit in which we obey them.

Jesus saw that the commandments were interpreted in a very negative way which led to minimalism. He interpreted them in *a positive way*. For example, the fifth commandment says, 'Thou shalt not kill.' But he said, 'You must love your neighbour.' The seventh commandment says, 'Thou shalt not steal.' But he said, 'You must share your goods with your neighbour when he is in need.'

He also saw that obedience was rooted in fear. He wanted it *rooted in love*. His whole relationship with his heavenly Father was based on love. When we love someone, we avoid doing anything to hurt that person.

For Jesus keeping the commandments was the bare minimum. This brings us to the most significant thing of all: he brought in a new and more exacting law – *the law of love*. Far from contradicting or abolishing the old law, the new law goes beyond it, and so brings it to perfection.

He said all of God's laws could be reduced to two: love of God and love of neighbour. These two, properly understood, include all the others. In a sense, then, there is only one law – the law of love. And there is only one sin – not to love.

REFLECTION — *Obedience leads to life*

It is sad to see neglected children. One of the most serious forms of neglect is when parents fail to guide their children – there are no rules, no values, no demands.

When parents care about their children, they have rules for them – not arbitrary rules, but reasonable ones which are explained to and accepted by the children. Their intention is not to make life miserable for their children. Quite the opposite. Their aim is to make life better for them, individually and collectively.

So it is with God's laws. God's laws are not his way of controlling his people and restricting their freedom. Their purpose is, as Moses pointed out to the people, 'that you may have life.' In short, they are meant to show his people the best way to live.

The fact that God took the trouble to give laws to his people was a sign of his love for them. If he didn't love them, he would have left them to their own devices. For their part, the people will show how much God means to them, and how wise they are, by observing his laws. His laws will give them guidance, and help them to live in harmony with one another.

Our attitude to God's laws is very important. If we see them as his way of controlling us, we will kick against them. But if we see them as a sign of his love for us, we will want to obey them. God's laws are not meant to curtail our freedom, but to help us to use it wisely. They are not a burden to be endured, but a source of life and wisdom. Those who obey God's laws walk with ease. Those who disobey his laws stumble and fall.

God wants us to have life, here and hereafter. To teach our children about God and his laws is again a sign of our love for them. Without that, what have we taught them? The whole purpose of life depends on it.

REFLECTION — *God's Law is a gift, not a burden*

The common theme of the readings is the Law of God. It is not God who needs laws; it is we who need them. As human beings we need moral boundaries. A world without limits would be a world of chaos. God's laws (or commandments) give us boundaries. By restraining our human waywardness they protect us from error and evil.

The purpose of God's law is not to constrain us, but to show us how to live. God's laws are not so much a set of rules as a set of values to live by. The Commandments are a map of life for a people who enjoy a special relationship with God. They should be seen as a gift, not a burden.

Keeping the commandments is the first thing. But we have to keep them in the right spirit. The Pharisees kept all the rules yet Jesus found serious fault with them. Our obedience must be motivated not by fear but by love. We don't keep the Commandments so that God will love us; we keep the Commandments *because* God loves us.

How easy things are for those who walk in the right way. The Lord's way is the right way. The Lord's way is straight, and the upright walk in it.

On the other hand, how difficult things are for those who walk in the wrong way. Those who walk in the wrong way bring a lot of trouble on themselves. The way of sinners is crooked; sinners stumble and fall.

Jesus did not come to abolish the Commandments. He came to take us beyond them. Therefore, it is no longer good enough to look at the Ten Commandments in the light of the Old Testament. As Christians we must approach the Commandments in the light of the Gospel. Jesus' teaching goes much farther than the Ten Commandments. He brought in a new and more exacting law- the law of love. He effectively reduced the commandments to two: love of God and love of neighbour.

Christians must not live by the Ten Commandments but by the 'law' of Jesus.

PRAYER OF THE FAITHFUL

Celebrant: Let us now open our hearts in prayer to the God who guides us by means of his commandments.

Response: Lord, hear our prayer.

Reader(s): For all Christians: that they may live their lives according to the values of the Gospel. [Pause] Let us pray to the Lord.

For those who make and enforce our laws: that they may be guided by the wisdom that comes from God. [Pause] Let us pray to the Lord.

For neglected children, and for prisoners. [Pause] Let us pray to the Lord.

For all gathered here: that we may have the kind of relationship with God which makes obeying his commandments natural and easy. [Pause] Let us pray to the Lord.

For our own special needs. [Longer pause] Let us pray to the Lord.

Celebrant: God of mercy, strengthen us in faith, hope, and love, so that we may be able to do with loving hearts what you ask of us. We make this prayer through Christ our Lord.

PRAYER/REFLECTION

The happiness of those who walk in God's way
is a recurrent theme in the Bible.
God's way is straight, and the upright walk in it.
The way of sinners is crooked; sinners stumble and fall.
Lord, take the blindness from our eyes,
the weakness from our wills,
and the hardness from our hearts,
so that we may know the happiness of those
who walk in your way.

THURSDAY OF THIRD WEEK OF LENT

INTRODUCTION AND CONFITEOR

One of the things that brings good projects to a bad end is when divisions occur. As today's Gospel puts it: 'Any kingdom that is divided against itself cannot stand.' Our world is full of divisions. Let us turn to the Lord and ask him to help us to heal our divisions. [Pause]

Lord Jesus, you came to reconcile us to one another and to the Father. Lord, have mercy.

Lord Jesus, you heal the wounds of sin and division. Christ have mercy.

Lord Jesus, you intercede for us with the Father. Lord, have mercy.

SCRIPTURE NOTE

In the *First Reading* (Jer 7:23-28) Jeremiah speaks of the sinful state of God's people. This is manifested in their stubborn refusal to listen to what God was saying to them through the numerous prophets he sent them. That same stubbornness of heart is evident in the *Gospel* (Lk 11:14-23), in the refusal of the religious leaders to believe in Jesus.

Jesus manifested his power by casting out a devil from a man who was dumb. The question arose: Where did his power come from? The ordinary people had no doubt but that it came from God. The religious leaders, however, perversely claimed that it came from the devil. Jesus shows them just how illogical they are, answering their charge with three arguments.

Firstly, the devil is not such a fool as to foster civil war among his servants. Secondly, there are other exorcists besides himself, who know that Satan's minions can be overpowered only by God's strength, and who therefore convict his critics of blasphemous slander. Thirdly, his detractors should know that the only power capable of breaking the grip of Satan is the power of God, and should draw the unavoidable conclusion that Satan's kingdom is being invaded by the kingdom of God.

REFLECTION — *Harden not your hearts*

In today's responsorial psalm the psalmist says to God's people: 'O that today you would listen to his voice! Harden not your hearts.'

We see an example of hardness of heart in the First Reading. There Jeremiah upbraids the people for their stubborn refusal to listen to what God was saying to them through the numerous prophets he sent them.

And in the Gospel we see that same stubbornness of heart in the refusal of the religious leaders to believe in Jesus. What is at stake is the source of Jesus' healing power. While the ordinary people recognised the God-given nature of Jesus' power, the religious leaders perversely claimed that he was in league with the devil. Jesus tried to reason with them. But it was no use – they had hardened their hearts against him.

To adopt a hard-hearted attitude is to maim oneself. A hard heart is a closed heart, so it can't receive. A hard heart inevitably becomes a barren heart. From a spiritual point of view, hardness of heart is one of the worst things that can happen to anyone.

It is to the heart that the call of God comes. God longs for our hearts, and is continually calling us into communion with him and with one another. Unfortunately, the heart is not always receptive. Some hearts are so hard that God's call makes no impression on them.

'Harden not your hearts,' says the psalmist. We would do well to heed those words. Jesus came, not just to purify our hearts, but to soften and warm them, so that they might be able to receive the word of God. Softened by the rain of his grace, and warmed by the sun of his love, the seed of God's word can take root in our hearts, and turn them from a desert into a garden.

REFLECTION — *The divided kingdom*

Jesus said that a kingdom which is divided cannot stand. We see what trouble there is when a country is divided, or when a family is divided. But in truth, each of us is a divided Kingdom – we are part light and part darkness. Even though this is an obvious truth, it can take a long time to grasp it. It is a humbling truth, yet there is a kind of freedom in knowing and accepting it.

The reality is that everyone is a mixture of light and shadow, good and evil. Each human heart is a divided kingdom. The sooner we come to terms with this the better. If the heart was completely unified it would make life very simple. But it is not. There is a war going on inside us, between altruism and egoism, between good and evil.

This is what Paul was talking about when he said very candidly: 'I do not understand my own behaviour; I fail to carry out the things I want to do, and I find myself doing the very things I hate' (Romans 7:15).

We have to face the fact that we are never the complete masters of ourselves. We are involved in a constant struggle. But struggle is good for us. It awakens and brings out all that is precious within us. Cheap victories do little for us. Good appears most vividly in resistance to its opposite. That is what heroism is about.

Because of this division we cannot afford to be complacent. We must go on striving for unity even though we may never attain it here on earth.

REFLECTION — *Invisible handicaps*

The man in the Gospel story was physically handicapped – he was dumb. Those who are physically handicapped know it. And outsiders know it too, and generally are sympathetic. The dumb man recognised his handicap, put his faith in Jesus, and was cured.

But he is not the only handicapped person in the story. Take the religious leaders. While the ordinary people recognised the God-given nature of Jesus' power, the religious leaders put a horrible 'spin' on what he had done. They perversely claimed that it was through the power of the devil that he had cured the dumb man. This shows that they too were handicapped, handicapped by the attitude they adopted towards Jesus – an attitude of wilful blindness and hardness of heart.

There are other kinds of handicaps besides physical ones. In some ways these other handicaps are more serious, because they are not so visible as the physical ones. Often those who are so afflicted are not aware of their condition, and so are not likely to seek a cure. Think of peoples' fears, selfishness, pride, smugness, prejudice, inability to see or to listen, and so on.

In truth, all of us are handicapped in some way. Each of us has an innate capacity to love. Unfortunately, this love often goes unexpressed. We have hands and we don't give, eyes and we don't see, ears and we don't hear, tongues and we don't speak, feelings and we don't show them.

The greatest handicap of all, however, is a crippled heart. A paraplegic observed: 'Living as a cripple in a wheelchair allows you to see more clearly the crippled hearts of some people whose bodies are whole and whose minds are sound.'

We should pray for the courage to acknowledge the handicaps we have. Recognition is the first step towards rehabilitation.

PRAYER OF THE FAITHFUL

Celebrant: Let us now bring our needs before God, confident that he will listen to us because we pray in the name of his Son.

Response: Lord, graciously hear us.

Reader(s): For unity in the Church and among the followers of Christ of different denominations. [Pause] Lord, hear us.

For unity among the nations of the world. [Pause] Lord, hear us.

For unity in families. [Pause] Lord, hear us.

For all in this congregation: that each of us may strive to be a source of unity among our friends and neighbours. [Pause] Lord, hear us.

For grace to be delivered from hardness of heart. [Pause] Lord, hear us.

For our own special needs. [Longer pause] Let us pray to the Lord.

Celebrant: Lord, in your gentle mercy, guide our wayward hearts, for we know that by ourselves we cannot please you. We make this prayer through Christ our Lord.

BEING WITH CHRIST

Jesus said: 'Whoever is not with me is against me.'

I sometimes feel that I live in a twilight world,

halfway between light and darkness.

I sometimes feel that I am in a state of indifference,

halfway between love and hate.
I sometimes feel I am trudging along a narrow little path,
halfway between good and evil.
Lord, save us from the illusion that because
we are not against you we are therefore with you.
Above all, save us from being neutral.

FRIDAY OF THIRD WEEK OF LENT

INTRODUCTION AND CONFITEOR

Today's Gospel reminds us of the two great commandments:
love of God and love of neighbour. The only real failure for a
Christian is the failure to love. Let us reflect on this for a moment. [Pause]

Lord Jesus, you help us to come back to you with all our hearts.
Lord, have mercy.

You take away all our iniquity so that we may have happiness
again. Christ, have mercy.

You let your mercy fall like dew on us. Lord, have mercy.

SCRIPTURE NOTE

The *First Reading* (Hos 14:2-10) contains an appeal to Israel
to turn away from idolatry and to come back to God. If she re-
pents of her infidelity and disloyalty, she will be treated with
great compassion. What comes across here is God's great love
for his people. If Israel responds to this love she will flourish in
beauty and plenty.

In the *Gospel* (Mk 12:28-34) Jesus tells us what the two most
important of God's commandments are. By rabbinical count,
the Law consisted of some 613 commandments. The Scribe's
question as to which commandment was the greatest was one
frequently discussed among the rabbis. Jesus was asked to name
one, but responded by naming two. Both are found in the Old
Testament; the first in Deuteronomy 6:4, the second in Leviti-

cus 19:18.

What Jesus did was to put the two together, thus emphasising their essential relatedness. No rabbi had previously done this. The emphasis on love became for Christians the identifying characteristic of their religion.

The Scribe agreed fully with Jesus, and went on to declare that true love of God and loving service of others are more important than elaborate cult. Nowhere else in the Gospel does a Scribe emerge in such a favourable light.

REFLECTION — *The two great commandments*

There was a man who regarded himself as a good Christian. He took special pride in his love for God, a love demonstrated by the fact that he had never deliberately missed going to church on Sunday. And he also took a quiet pride in his love for his neighbours, a love demonstrated by the fact that he had never quarrelled with any of them.

However, you only had to talk to his neighbours to know that he didn't really love them. If the truth was told, he was indifferent to them. He had shown no solidarity with them in their struggles, had offered no comfort to them in their losses, had never put himself out to help them in their need. His love for his neighbour was an illusion. And so was his love of God, because one can't claim to love God while being indifferent to one's neighbours.

He had separated the two commandments, something that is clean contrary to the Gospel. The two commandments are essentially related: true love of neighbour springs from love of God, and true love of God express itself in love of neighbour.

In practice it often happens that the two commandments are separated. Those who have faith often have no love, and those who love often have no faith. Thus the Gospel is torn in two.

Jesus spoke of two great commandments. The first – that we should love God. The second – that we should love our neighbour.

He didn't say that they were the same thing, but that they are like two sides of the one coin. If we want the total Gospel we must have both. He himself showed us how to do this.

Natural love extends only to individuals with whom we feel united by reason of blood, or tribe, or common interest. Christian love, however, knows no boundaries.

REFLECTION — *Becoming a loving person*

Near the end of her life, Marilyn Monroe held the following conversation with her maid, Lena.

'Nobody's ever going to love me now, Lena. And I don't blame them. What am I good for? I can't have children. I can't cook. I've been divorced three times. Who would want me?'

'Oh, lots of men would want you,' Lena replied.

'Yes,' said Marylin, 'lots of men would *want* me. But who would *love* me?'

Sadly, the answer was probably 'nobody'. Marylin had lots of fans, and lots of men who were willing to use her. But she had no one *to love her for herself.*

Love is at the heart of today's scripture readings. In the First Reading we see God's love for his people. And in the Gospel Jesus tells us that the two most important commandments both have to do with love.

Many people make the same mistake as Marylin Monroe. They see the problem of love as *being loved* rather than *being a loving person*. Hence, all their efforts go into making themselves loveable through being successful, or glamorous, or powerful, or rich ... And so they end up without love, because they are loved, not for themselves, but for something they possess. On the other hand, if they became loving people, they would be loved, and loved for themselves.

In the end, all of us want to be loved, not for our achievements, or talents, or possessions, but for ourselves. This is precisely how God loves his people as today's First Reading clearly shows. And this is how God loves each one of us, and how he wants us to love one another.

Jesus exhorts us to open their hearts to God and to our neighbours. In so doing, he is not laying a burden on us. He is calling us to life. To open one's heart is to begin to live. Besides, a loving heart is a joyful heart.

REFLECTION — *Love is more important than sacrifice*

Jesus said that the two greatest commandments were: that we should love God with our whole heart .. and that we should love our neighbour as ourselves. The Scribe agreed fully with Jesus, and went on to declare: 'This is far more important than any holocaust or sacrifice.' In other words, love of God and loving service of our neighbours are more important than elaborate cult.

This would have endeared the Scribe to Jesus because he himself had said (quoting Hosea 6:6): 'What I want is mercy, not sacrifice' (Matthew 9:13). This is a recurrent theme in the prophets. (Isaiah 1:11ff. is a powerful example).

The prophets upbraided the people for not bringing their lives into conformity with their worship. We have already seen that God is not impressed by a fasting that is divorced from justice and concern for the poor and the needy.

We too are challenged to bring our lives into conformity with our faith and worship. To offer sacrifice to God is a great thing. But to show mercy to a fellow human being is an even greater thing. And it is harder, especially when the person in question deserves to be punished, and when it is in our power to do so.

When we offer a sacrifice to God there is an immediate payback: we feel good that we have done something worthwhile and chalked up some merit. But when we show mercy to a fellow human being often there is no pay-back.

One thing should be a big help to us, namely, the conviction that we ourselves stand in daily need of God's mercy. And we should remember the words of Jesus: 'Blessed are the merciful; they shall have mercy shown them.'

It is tragic to find religious people devoid of the chief human attribute – compassion for others. But when a person combines true religion and deep compassion, you have a powerful combination. Here you have true holiness.

PRAYER OF THE FAITHFUL

Celebrant: Mindful of the two commandments of love, we now bring our needs before God.

Response: Lord, hear us in your love.

Reader(s): For all Christians: that they may live out in their lives the two commandments of love. [Pause] We pray in faith.

For the world in which we live: that love and peace may prevail over hatred and violence. [Pause] We pray in faith.

For the sick and the needy: that through our love they may know that God cares about them. [Pause] We pray in faith.

For this community: that our celebration of the Eucharist may strengthen our unity and deepen our love for one another. [Pause] We pray in faith.

For our own special needs. [Longer pause] We pray in faith.

Celebrant: All-loving God, help us to make love the foundation of our lives. May our love for you express itself in our eagerness to do good to others. We ask this through Christ our Lord.

PRAYER

Lord, open our hearts when they are closed,
soften them when they are hard,
warm them when they are cold,
fill them when they are empty,
heal them when they are wounded,
and mend them when they are broken,
so that we, your disciples, may bear the fruits of love.

SATURDAY OF THIRD WEEK OF LENT

INTRODUCTION AND CONFITEOR

Two men went into the Temple to pray. One boasted that he was not a sinner like other people. The other acknowledged that he was a sinner, and asked God to be merciful to him. Let us now call to mind our sins, and ask God to turn his face from our sins, but not from us. [Pause]

Lord Jesus, you blot out our sins. Lord, have mercy.

You give us again the joy of your help. Christ, have mercy.

You put a steadfast spirit within us. Lord, have mercy.

SCRIPTURE NOTE

At the time of Hosea, religion in Israel had become shallow and loveless. In the *First Reading* (Hos 5:15–6:6) the prophet exposes the insincerity of the people's repentance. He points out how short-lived their declarations of fidelity are. They still count on external cult without submitting themselves to God's commands. What God wants from them is love, not sacrifice.

The parable of the Pharisee and the Tax Collector (*Gospel*, Lk 18:9-14) was aimed at those who prided themselves on being virtuous and despised everyone else. It contrasts the proud attitude of the Pharisee with the humble attitude of the tax collector.

The Pharisee thinks that because of his good works God owes him salvation. He doesn't regard himself as a sinner at all. Therefore, he has no realisation of his need of grace and forgiveness. The tax collector knows he's a sinner. So he throws himself on the mercy of God. His humble prayer wins him forgiveness.

The Pharisee entered the Temple with a false sense of his own virtue, and left it in that same illusory state. The tax collector entered the Temple with a deep sense of his own sinfulness, and left it with a profound sense of the goodness of God.

REFLECTION — *Where the Pharisee went wrong*

The Pharisee in Jesus' story was not a scoundrel. In fact, he was an honest, faithful, family man, and a meticulous observer of the Law. He did even more than the Law required of him. It required only one fast a year (on the Day of Atonement), but he fasted twice a week. It required tithes only on certain commodities, but he paid tithes on everything.

Where then did he go wrong?

He went wrong firstly in his attitude to God. Since he didn't consider himself a sinner, he felt no need of God's mercy. Quite the opposite. He believed that he had run up a formidable credit-balance with God. Which meant that he had got God in his debt.

And he went wrong secondly in his attitude to others. He despised others.

What we see in the Pharisee is arrogant self-reliance, complacency, and scorn of the sinner. He was without a trace of humility. And humility is the soil in which all other virtues flourish.

He considered himself a holy man because of the considerable sacrifices he made, such as fasting and tithing. But when it came to love, he was woefully lacking. In the final analysis, it is love that counts. God said through the prophet Hosea, 'What I want is love, not sacrifice.' There can be no holiness without love.

The prayer of the tax collector is a model. He said simply, 'Lord, be merciful to me I am a sinner.' In saying this, he was simply telling the truth. This is a prayer that God cannot fail to hear.

If we sincerely pray this prayer, it will keep us in right relationship with God and with our fellow human beings.

REFLECTION — *Confessing our own sins*

One of the mistakes the Pharisee made was to confess the sins of others rather than his own. In his view, other people were all thieves, rogues, and adulterers. He, on the other hand, was a virtuous man. He fasted twice a week, and gave a tenth of his annual income for the support of the priests and the upkeep of the Temple.

The Pharisee didn't consider himself a sinner at all. Consequently, he felt no need of God's mercy. But he was a sinner. In fact, he had some very serious sins of attitude. He was proud, self-righteousness, and despised others. But he was blind to these sins.

Nothing so blinds us to our own sins as a preoccupation with the sins of others. And the more preoccupied we are with the sins of others, the less likely we are to do anything about our own. There are few things that give as much satisfaction to the ego as pointing out the mistakes and faults of others.

This is a trap into which any of us can fall. It is easy to get worked up about the sins of another, but a psychological wall prevents us from seeing our own. We must take the beam out of our own eye first, and then we can think about removing the splinter from our neighbour's eye.

The tax collector shows us the way to go. He concentrated on his own sins, and left the sins of others between them and God. His words were few, but his attitude was right. He didn't draw up a list of his sins. He did something better. He declared, 'I am a sinner.'

We should follow his example. Even though we may not be conscious of any specific sins, we can still say in all truth, 'I am a sinner.'

'Lord, be merciful to me, a sinner.' We should make this prayer our own. If we sincerely pray this prayer, it will keep us in right relationship with God and with our fellow human beings.

REFLECTION — *When we enter a church*

When we enter a church we are conscious of coming before God. And to come before God is to be humbled. In the presence of God we become acutely aware of God's greatness and our insignificance. And we realise that whereas God is all-perfect, we are sinful creatures. How then can anyone come before

God and dare to look down on anyone else?

In the house of God entitlements count for nothing, and privilege is blown away like smoke before the wind. But when we let go of those things that give us a false sense of superiority, and which separate us from others, a beautiful thing happens. We find that we are exalted, just as Jesus said. We begin to realise our true greatness, which lies, not in ourselves, but in God. Our greatness lies in the fact that we are children of God.

Before God all of us are equal. It is not that we are all reduced to the lowest common denominator. No. It is that we are all raised up. We are like people set on a mountain top. On a mountain top to speak of higher and lower places would be silly.

The Pharisee entered the Temple with a false sense of his own virtue, and left it in that same illusory state. The tax collector entered the Temple with a deep sense of his own sinfulness, and left it with a profound sense of the goodness of God.

We cannot pray properly unless the heart is right. The heart of the Pharisee was not right; it was full of pride, and full of himself. The heart of the tax collector was right; it was humble, open, and receptive.

We should make our own the prayer of the tax collector: 'Lord, be merciful to me, a sinner.' If we sincerely pray that prayer, it will keep us in right relationship with God and with our fellow human beings. And it will enable us to grasp, with tranquil hearts, both our grandeur and our insignificance in the world.

PRAYER OF THE FAITHFUL

Celebrant: God hears the prayers of the humble. Let us now bring our petitions before him with humility and confidence.

Response: Lord, hear our prayer.

Reader(s): That our churches may be places where sinners can experience the tender mercy of God. [Pause] Let us pray to the Lord.

For tax collectors and all those who do unpopular but necessary jobs. [Pause] Let us pray to the Lord.

For each other and for ourselves: that we may never look down on others or belittle their dignity. [Pause] Let us pray to the Lord.

For grace to remember that what God wants from us is not sacrifice but love. [Pause] Let us pray to the Lord.

For our own special needs. [Longer pause] Let us pray to the Lord.

Celebrant: Lord, give us the courage to acknowledge our sins, the wisdom to learn from them, and the generosity of heart to extend to others the compassion we desire for ourselves. We make this prayer through Christ our Lord.

REFLECTION
There are people who still think like the Pharisee.
They maintain that the Church is for saints not sinners.
But that would result in a very small church,
and would make as little sense as a hospital
that accepted only healthy people.
We go to church not because we think we are saints
but because we know we are sinners.
We are humble enough to admit our sinfulness,
but brave enough to strive for something better..

Fourth Week of Lent

MONDAY OF FOURTH WEEK OF LENT

INTRODUCTION AND CONFITEOR
Our faith is the most precious thing we have. However, it is not always as strong and as active as it might be. So let us turn to God, and ask him to strengthen our faith, and help us to express it in service of others. [Pause]

Lord, Jesus you are our light and our help. Lord, have mercy.
You are the stronghold of our lives. Christ, have mercy.

You lead us in the path of eternal life. Lord, have mercy.

SCRIPTURE NOTE

From here on (with the exception of Wednesday in Holy Week) the Gospel is taken from St John. In these extracts John outlines the swiftly developing crisis between Jesus and the Jews. He makes it clear that the conflict was about a final theological judgement that people have to pass on Jesus: Is he, or is he not, the Son of the Father, sent by him into the world for its salvation? Some of these passages are difficult. Consequently, the Scripture Note may be a little longer.

The *First Reading* of today's Mass (Is 65:17-21) is the kind of reading we associate more with Advent than with Lent. In it the prophet offers hope to the exiles who returned from Babylon, and were disappointed at the harsh conditions of life in their homeland. The *Gospel* (Jn 4:43-54) shows the new creation promised by Isaiah being inaugurated by Jesus – for those who have faith in him.

Despite some notable differences, it seems that John's story of the cure of official's son is the same story as the curing of the centurion's servant which we find in the synoptics (Mt 8:5-13; Lk 7:1-10).

The official obviously had heard of the 'signs' that Jesus had performed in Jerusalem. Jesus seems at first to question the faith of the official, suggesting that he needs to see signs and wonders in order to believe. Jesus is making the point that such faith is inadequate. He challenges the official to go beyond the need to see signs and wonders.

This is not to say that true faith cannot find any place for the miraculous, but that faith that cannot believe without a miracle is deficient. The official then moves to a deeper faith. Now the word of Jesus is enough for him. And his faith is rewarded with the cure of his son. And all his household come to believe too. This shows how faith is transmitted from person to person.

REFLECTION — *The lamp of faith*

One night I saw a motorist driving along a busy road oblivious of the fact that he had no lights on. Motorists going in the opposite direction tried to warn him by flashing their lights, but he didn't seem to notice, or if he did, he took no heed. He kept on going at speed, happily and safely – at least for the time being.

How did he manage to get by without lights? The answer is very simple. The road along which he was travelling was a well-lit one, so strictly speaking he didn't need the lights. But sooner or later he would find himself on some dark back road. Then he would realise his lack of lights, and would reach for the switch. Hopefully the lights would come on immediately.

In good times we may think that we have a strong faith. It's only in times of trial that we discover whether the lamp of faith is a beacon or just a lowly candle which the first gust of wind threatens to extinguish.

The man who came to Jesus had some faith. But it seems that he needed signs and wonders in order to believe. Jesus challenged him to believe without signs. He asked him to accept his word. To his credit, the man responded positively. He went away relying solely on the word of Jesus. In the end he was doubly blessed. Not only was his son cured, but he himself had come to a stronger and deeper faith – a faith which his whole household shared in.

At the end of the day all we have is the word of Jesus. To live by his word is to live by faith.

REFLECTION — *Trusting his word*

In one of the temptations the devil took Jesus to the pinnacle of the Temple in Jerusalem, and said to him: 'If you are the Son of God, throw yourself down; for scripture says, "He will give his angels charge of you; they will support you on their hands in case you hurt your foot against a stone."' But Jesus said, 'Scripture also says, "You must not put the Lord your God to the test."'

This was the temptation to do something spectacular in order to elicit faith. The devil was right in suggesting that faith involves a leap. But not the kind of leap he suggested. It involves a leap of trust. To have faith doesn't mean we have all the answers. Here on earth there is no such thing as absolute certainty about spiritual things.

This temptation was repeated many times in the course of Jesus' public ministry. People demanded signs and wonders before they would believe. But Jesus refused to provide them. To give in to those demands would be to cheapen faith. Faith is not magic. The person who asks for proof has not learnt the meaning of faith.

We have an example of this in today's Gospel. It seems that the official needed to see signs and wonders in order to believe. Jesus challenged him to go beyond the need to see signs and wonders. To his credit, the official rose to the challenge. He placed his trust in the word of Jesus. Thus he came to a deeper faith. And his faith was rewarded with the cure of his son. And all his hold come to believe too.

How many people are there whose word we would trust absolutely? The answer is, 'Very few.' The word of Jesus is different from the word of anyone else. It carries an authority which no other word carries. At the end of the day all we have is the word of Jesus. To live by his word is to live by faith.

REFLECTION — *Faith and miracles*

It's clear that the official who came to Jesus had some faith. But it would seem that like many of Jesus' contemporaries he was a 'sign-believer'. In other words, his faith depended on seeing signs and wonders. Jesus challenged him to believe without signs.

To his credit, the official was equal to the challenge. And so he moved to a deeper faith. Now the word of Jesus was enough for him. And his faith was rewarded with the cure of his son. And all his household come to believe too. This shows how faith is transmitted from person to person.

It is a poor faith that needs signs and wonders to sustain it. Faith is the belief that what we see is not all. Faith is not knowledge of what the mystery of the universe is, but the conviction that there is a mystery – a mystery that is greater than us, and that is not subject to human understanding.

Those who are attuned to God do not need to see signs and wonders. They are conscious of living in a world which is sustained by his power, and every part of which speaks of him. And yet the 'miracles' are there in daily life if only people would open their eyes.

Those whose faith must be nourished by extraordinary occurrences are like people depending on the odd snack here and there. Those who are able to nourish their faith from the daily 'miracles' that surround them are like people sitting at a banquet table.

PRAYER OF THE FAITHFUL

Celebrant: As we come to God with our needs, let us draw inspiration from the faith of the court official, and from Jesus' response to that faith.

Response: Lord, hear our prayer.

Reader(s): For Christians: that their lives may bear witness to the faith they profess with their lips. [Pause] Let us pray to the Lord.

For non-believers: that the example of Christians may help them to come to faith. [Pause] Let us pray to the Lord.

For the sick and the lonely: that through our love they may know that God cares about them. [Pause] Let us pray to the Lord.

For all in this congregation: that we may nourish our faith through regular prayer. [Pause] Let us pray to the Lord.

For our own special needs. [Longer pause] Let us pray to the Lord.

Celebrant: God of love and mercy, sustain our faith when things are difficult, so that we may have the strength to persevere in goodness. We make this prayer through Christ our Lord.

SIGNS

At the end of the day all we have is the word of Jesus.
But, like the offical in the Gospel story,
that ought to be enough for us.
Lord, give us the kind of faith in your promises
that will enable us to live out joyfully
the mystery of our fragile human condition,
which sees us suspended between earth and heaven,
between time and eternity,
between nothingness and infinity.

TUESDAY OF FOURTH WEEK OF LENT

INTRODUCTION AND CONFITEOR

Of all the commodities with which our earth has been blessed water is the most precious. In today's readings water is used as a symbol of God's blessings to his people. We think especially of the waters of Baptism, through which we received a share in the life of God. [Pause]

Lord Jesus, in the waters of Baptism you give us a share in your own divine life. Lord, have mercy.

You quench our thirst with the living water of your grace. Christ, have mercy.

You lead us to the springs of eternal life. Lord, have mercy.

SCRIPTURE NOTE

Both readings are concerned with life-giving water. In the *First Reading* (Ezek 47:1-9.12) the prophet Ezekiel talks about a vision in which he saw a stream of water flowing outwards from the Temple. As it goes it swells into a river, and everywhere it flows it brings health and life. This is an image of the blessings

God is offering to his people. The *Gospel* (Jn 5:1-3.5-16) shows that God's blessings now flow to his people in and through the person of Jesus.

The healing pool John talks about was no doubt a natural phenomenon. The pool bubbled up when the intermittent underground spring that fed it became more active, and was thought to be especially curative at those times. Gathered by the poolside was a collection of unfortunates. John doesn't tell us why, from all of these, Jesus singled out one man. However, he does underline that his case was especially pitiable; he had been ill for thirty-eight years.

But John is interested in the miracle only as a sign of Jesus' power. Without any reference to the water, Jesus heals the man. This shows that water is now superceded by the word and action of Jesus. The miracle is a symbol of the healing and life God is offering his people in and through Jesus.

The cure precipitated a row with the Jewish leaders. Instead of welcoming the fact that a poor man was made well, they criticise him for carrying his mat on the Sabbath. In this we see their legal rigidity. Legalists think only of the law, and not of the people for whom the law was made. They directed their complaint, not against Jesus, but against the man who had been cured. His defence was: If Jesus could perform a cure like this, then surely it was proper to obey his command.

Regarding the words: 'Do not sin any more, or something worse may happen to you', Jesus is not saying that the man's sins were responsible for his affliction. The 'something worse' refers to the spiritual 'illness' that sin causes.

The man was probably acting in good faith when he reported to the Jews that it was Jesus who cured him: he was simply answering the question they had put to him earlier. In any case, it meant trouble for Jesus, as we will see.

REFLECTION — *Life-giving water*
Both of today's readings have life-giving water as their main

theme. The chief property of water is to give life. This is beautifully illustrated in the First Reading. There we read of a stream of water that flows outwards from the Temple, and brings life everywhere it flows. The life-giving water symbolises the blessings God is offering to his people.

The Gospel tells of a man who was crippled for thirty-eight years. Day in and day out, he sat by the side of a pool of water in the hope of being cured. It was all in vain until the day he encountered Jesus. Without any reference to the water, Jesus healed the man. And he was able to take up his mat and walk away.

This shows that water is now superseded by the word and action of Jesus. The miracle is a symbol of the healing and life God is offering his people in and through Jesus.

What happened to the man reminds us of what happened to us in baptism. On the day of our baptism we were brought to a font. There we had blessed water poured over us. The purpose of the water was not just to cleanse us of sin but to give us new life – a share in the life of God. And we began to walk in the freedom of the children of God.

We are halfway through Lent. The purpose of Lent is to help us to live our baptism more fully. Now we will bless some water and sprinkle it over ourselves. It will remind us of the life-giving waters of baptism, and renew the grace of baptism within us.

Prayer over the water

My dear brothers and sisters, this water will be used to remind us of our baptism. Let us ask God to bless it, and to keep us faithful to our baptismal calling.

Lord God, creator and sustainer of all life, we ask you to bless + this water. Your Spirit descended on Jesus at his baptism in the Jordan, and accompanied him into the desert. May the same Spirit descend on us now, and accompany us on our Lenten journey. We ask this through the same Christ our Lord.

(The priest now sprinkles himself and the people with the water.)

REFLECTION — *Wanting to get well*

Jesus said to the paralysed man, 'Do you want to be well?' It seemed a needless question. Was it not clear that he wanted to get well? Perhaps not. He had been crippled for 38 years, and by now was completely dependent on others. To be cured would mean managing on his own. So it was just possible that he might not want to be cured because of the changes it would bring about in his life.

But he did want to be cured, and let Jesus know it. Then Jesus said to him. 'Get up, pick up his sleeping mat and walk'. 'Get up!' That was the thing he most desired but was least able to do. But at the word of Jesus he did it. The effort to get up was part of his cure.

Prior to his cure, the man was stuck in a hole. We too can get stuck in a hole. However, we can become so comfortable in our habits that we cannot contemplate living differently. If we want the power of Jesus to be effective we must sincerely want to change. And we must be willing to play a part in our recovery. The power of God never dispenses with human effort. Miracles happen only when our will and God's power co-operate to make them possible.

There are many things in life which defeat us. But when we have the desire and determination to make the effort, the power of God gets its opportunity, and with God we can conquer what for long has conquered us.

Sometimes a cure may not be possible. The challenge then is to carry one's cross with dignity. One has to be content to hobble along the road with humility and patience. Such people will never win a race. But by their courage and dignity they will make grace visible in the world. And they will give the rest of us courage to risk standing up, by the grace of God, and limping along our path.

REFLECTION — *The compassion of Jesus*

A doctor tells how he spent ten years listening to the cries of patients suffering from kidney stones. Then one night he found himself lying on a stretcher, screaming, in the emergency room of a hospital. 'I had no idea what the pain was like until I experienced it myself,' he said. He says that he now prescribes much stronger medication to ease the searing pain. And he tells his patients, 'I know what you're going through.'

That doctor had to get ill himself before he could understand the pain his patients were suffering. But there are some people who are so sensitive that they are able to understand the pain of others without having to suffer it themselves.

Jesus was like that. We can tell from the way he dealt with the man who was lying by the poolside. As soon as he saw him, his heart went out to him. And the man's long agony was over.

Now look at how the religious leaders dealt with the same man. When they saw him walking about, instead of being happy for him, they accused him of breaking the Sabbath by carrying his sleeping mat. How their cold and legalistic attitude contrasts with the warm and compassionate attitude of Jesus.

The man in the Gospel had been waiting by the pool at Bethzatha for 38 years. Why did he have to wait so long? Because he had no one to help him. Hospital waiting lists are a big issue today. People have died while on waiting lists.

We marvel at the people who brought the man to the pool each day. It seemed so futile. Yet they did it. It gave him hope. It took him out of the house. We think of those who care for the sick, especially those who are bed-ridden and terminally ill.

Jesus, the friend of the friendless, invites us to be sensitive to the needs of others. And may our own encounters with suffering help us to empathise with other sufferers.

PRAYER OF THE FAITHFUL

Celebrant: Let us pray with confidence to God who alone can quench our deepest thirst.

Response: Lord, hear our prayer.

Reader(s): For all the baptised: that they may live out their calling to be other Christs in the world. [Pause] Let us pray to the Lord.

For those who administer our health service. [Pause] Let us pray to the Lord.

For the sick: that they may know God's comforting. [Pause] Let us pray to the Lord.

For those who work for the sick: that God may bless them with warm hearts and sensitive hands. [Pause] Let us pray to the Lord.

For all gathered here: that if we are in stuck in some kind of a rut, we may seek the help we need to get out of it. [Pause] Let us pray to the Lord.

For our own special needs. [Longer pause] Let us pray to the Lord.

Celebrant: Heavenly Father, you sent your Son into our world to bring the good news of salvation to the poor. Make us his disciples envoys of your love to the world. We ask this through the same Christ our Lord.

REFLECTION

There are many vocations in the Church.
But the most important vocation of all
is the vocation we received at baptism, namely,
the vocation to be a disciple of Jesus.
Every time we enter a church
and sign ourselves with holy water,
we are reminding ourselves of our baptism,
and committing ourselves to live up to it.

WEDNESDAY OF FOURTH WEEK OF LENT

INTRODUCTION AND CONFITEOR

'At a favourable time I will answer you, on the day of salvation I will help you.' These lovely words, once addressed by God to his people, are now addressed to us. This a favourable time for us to turn to God. [Pause]

Lord Jesus, you are kind and full of compassion. Lord, have mercy.

You are slow to anger and abounding in love. Christ, have mercy.

You are faithful in all your words and loving in all your deeds. Lord, have mercy.

SCRIPTURE NOTE

The exiles in Babylon were feeling very low. And little wonder. Their kingdom had fallen. Jerusalem had been destroyed. The Temple had been reduced to rubble. Their sons and daughters had been taken into exile. So they asked themselves what had become of God's promises? They felt that God had forgotten them.

The prophet Isaiah (*First Reading*, Is 49:8-15) assures them that this is not so. God can no more abandoned his people than a mother can abandon her child. He tells them that their sorrows will soon end. God will bring their sons and daughters back from exile. He will level out a highway to facilitate their return. And there will be a great restoration.

The exiles did indeed come back. And even though the return fell short of the glowing picture painted here, it did point the way to the messianic era.

The *Gospel* (Jn 5:1 7-30) follows on from yesterday's. The Jews accuse Jesus of breaking the sabbath. Jesus says that God does not cease working on the sabbath. (The statement in Genesis 2:2 doesn't mean a literal cessation of God's creative activity, without which the world would cease to exist). Just as the Father is not inhibited by the sabbath law, neither is the Son. His opponents interpret this as meaning that he is making himself equal to God. Jesus goes on to insist on an absolute harmony of activity between Father and Son. He has come, not to do his own will, but the will of the Father who sent him.

They had seen him perform a great deed – the healing of the paralytic. But he tells them that they will see even greater things from him. One of these 'greater things' will be the raising of the dead to life. Since the powers of life and death belong only to God, Jesus is saying that he possesses this divine prerogative. This means not only the final resurrection, but the gift of new life in the here and now, the life of grace that is the beginning of the life of glory.

Another divine prerogative that Jesus possesses is that of judgement. Again, this judgement takes place not only at the end of time but in the here and now, on the basis of acceptance or rejection of Jesus.

REFLECTION — *Doing the will of God*

There was a rabbi who had a great reputation for sanctity. One day a stranger arrived from a faraway town to see him. On his arrival the stranger was introduced to one of the rabbi's disciples.

'We have heard that your rabbi is a very holy man,' the stranger said. 'Well, we have a rabbi in our town who is also very close to God?'

'How can you tell that?' the disciple asked.

'Because he works miracles,' the stranger replied. 'What miracles has your rabbi performed?'

'There are miracles and miracles,' the disciple answered. 'It seems that the people of your town regard it as a miracle if God should do your rabbi's bidding. Well, we in this town regard it as a miracle that our rabbi does God's bidding.'

The message of this little story: holiness consists, not in getting God to do our will, but in getting ourselves to do God's will. False religion tries to manipulate God. True religion tries to serve God.

What was at the heart of Jesus' life and ministry? Today's Gospel give us a very clear answer. It was his relationship with his Father. He lived in a communion of mind and heart with the

Father. He submitted his will to the will of the Father, even though it led him to the cross.

We are called to share the intimacy of Jesus' relationship with the Father. It is what is offered to us in baptism. Jesus lived a life of complete obedience to the Father. This shows us the way to go. We must ask the Lord to increase our commitment to do his will, even if it is at the expense of our own agendas.

REFLECTION — *Can a mother forget her child?*

A mother's love is the most reliable human love that we have. Two examples. (One is enough at a time).

(1) A missionary Sister working in Africa tells of a woman who scarcely had any feet at all due to the ravages of leprosy. One day she noticed a spot on her young child. Taking the child in her arms, she somehow managed to walk six miles to the mission health clinic. 'Sister, my child has got leprosy,' she said. The Sister examined the child. It turned out that the spot was not leprosy after all. The woman took back the child, and walked all the way back home. She didn't even stop to rest, so happy was she on hearing that her child did not have leprosy.

(2) The name of Frederick Douglas will forever be associated with the struggle to abolish slavery in America. He grew up on a southern plantation, but eventually escaped. Against all the odds, he managed to get an education, and rose to a high position in American society. He was fortunate in that he had a wonderful mother. She was enslaved on a plantation eleven miles from her infant son. Yet after toiling a full day, she would walk those eleven miles to look at her sleeping child, hoping that he would sense a mother's love. Then she returned to the plantation in time to begin another day of labour.

Little wonder that the Bible uses a mother's love as an image of God's love for us. In today's First Reading we hear these lovely words: 'Can a woman forget her baby at the breast, feel no pity for the child she has borne? Even if these were to forget, I will not forget you,' says the Lord.

If a mother, who after all is a mere human being, is capable of such steadfast and self-sacrificing love, then how much greater is God's love for us who are his children. Even when we are in sin, God does not cease to love us.

We mustn't use that love as an excuse to live badly. Rather, it should be a spur to us to respond in kind. Jesus, who knew the love of the Father better than anyone else, sets us an example when he says, 'I seek to do not my own will, but the will of him who sent me.'

REFLECTION — *Eternal life*

There was an old and infirm man who lived in a shack on the edge of the forest. One winter's morning he got up to find only one meal of porridge left, the fireplace empty, and snow on the ground. He felt like asking God to take him to heaven there and then. However, he managed to summon up a little spirit, and went into the forest to collect firewood.

When he had collected a good bundle, he put a rope around it, tied a knot, only to find that he was unable to move it. With that he grew depressed, and looking up the heaven said, 'Lord, take me now. I've nothing left to live for.'

In an instant the Angel of Death was standing at his side, and said, 'You sent for me. Well, now that I'm here, what can I do for you?' Quick as a flash the old man replied, 'Hey son, would you ever give me a hand with this bundle of sticks.'

This little story shows that even though life may be difficult, it is still precious. But God intends us for something still more precious. He intends us for eternal life.

Today's Gospel tells us that eternal life comes through Jesus. He was sent by the Father so that we might have life, here and hereafter. Those who believe in him, and who do what he says, have passed from death to life.

Eternal life is not something that begins when we die. It has already begun in Baptism. Eternal life will merely be the full flowering of what we received in Baptism. We live our earthly lives under the brightness of immortality.

PRAYER OF THE FAITHFUL

Celebrant: Jesus came that we might have life both here and hereafter. Let us pray with confidence for all our needs.

Response: Lord, graciously hear us.

Reader(s): For the Church: that through its ministry it may give people an experience of the tender and steadfast love of God. [Pause} Lord, hear us.

For parents: that they may love their children in good times and in bad. [Pause} Lord, hear us.

For our own parents, who first gave us an experience of love. [Pause} Lord, hear us.

For all gathered here: that we express our love for God by trying to do his will at all times. [Pause} Lord, hear us.

For our own special needs. [Longer pause] Lord, hear us.

Celebrant: Father, your love even here on earth brings us the gifts of heaven. Guide us in this present life, and lead us to that unfailing light in which you have your dwelling. We ask this through Christ our Lord.

REFLECTION

'Can a woman forget her baby at the breast,
feel no pity for the child she has borne?
Even if these were to forget, I will not forget you,'
says the Lord.
A mother's love is the most reliable love that we have.
But since it is still human, it is imperfect and limited.
We all long for a love that is absolutely trustworthy.
Only God can give us what we are looking for.

THURSDAY OF FOURTH WEEK OF LENT

INTRODUCTION AND CONFITEOR

In today's First Reading we see how quickly the Israelites fell back into idolatry. Whenever anything usurps the place God should occupy, idolatry enters our life. Let us reflect for a moment to see what place God has in our lives. [Pause]

Lord Jesus, in your compassion you blot out our offences. Lord, have mercy.

You wash us from our guilt, and cleanse us from our sins. Christ, have mercy.

You create a pure heart for us, and put a steadfast spirit within us. Lord, have mercy.

SCRIPTURE NOTE

The *First Reading* (Ex 32:7-14) shows how the Israelites abandoned God and fell into idolatry. God reacts very angrily, threatening to destroy the wicked and form a new nation. However, Moses appeals to God on the people's behalf. He tells God that if he destroys the people, he will show himself up in a very unfavourable light to the pagan peoples. He asks God to remember the promises he made to Abraham, Isaac and Jacob. And God relents.

The incident seems to portray God as an angry, jealous God, who will resort to the most terrible punishments when his law is disobeyed. But that is not the message of the story. God's angry reaction is a warning, not a threat. God wants his people to realise the seriousness of their sin so that they will repent. His aim is to win back his people. And that is what happens.

The *Gospel* (Jn 5:31-47) follows on from yesterday's. Jesus is trying to convince the religious leaders that he has been sent by God. He is doing this, not for his own sake, but for their sake. He agrees that his own unsupported testimony to himself need not be true. But there are other witnesses.

The first witness is John the Baptist, whom they regarded as a shining light. John testified clearly that Jesus was sent by God (cf. John 1:29.36). The second witness is even greater – the works he does in the Father's name. These make it plain that his claim is justified. But there is a still greater witness – God himself. The Father who sent him has given testimony on his behalf. The Old Testament scriptures from Moses on testify on his behalf. They were leading to him.

In spite of all these witnesses, the religious leaders refuse to believe in him. Yet they are ready to believe any charlatan who comes along armed only with his own credentials. Jesus doesn't have to judge them; they stand denounced by their obduracy.

REFLECTION — *The threat of idolatry*

The greatest sign God gave the Israelites of his love for them was when he delivered them from slavery in Egypt. Sadly, as the First Reading shows, they quickly fell back into idolatry.

We might think that idolatry belongs to primitive peoples and to a bygone age. This is not so. Modern people have their idols too, and how they worship those idols! They may not get down on their knees before them, or offer sacrifices to them. But they worship them in other ways.

Whenever anything usurps the place God should occupy, then idolatry enters our life. Money is probably the most common idol today. But there are others – possessions, pleasure, success, fame, power ... A life based on the worship of things is a life of idolatry.

What is enthroned in our heart becomes the substance of our desires and the object of our strivings. In short, it becomes our god. We worship what we love.

Idolatry leads at best to a superficial life, and at worst to a debased life. But the greatest harm idolatry does is that it causes us to forget the true God.

Jesus shows us who God is, and how we can keep him at the centre of our lives. God is not some remote and uncaring figure. God is our heavenly Father, who is close to us, and to whom we are important and precious.

We must strive to keep God at the centre of our hearts. And we must try to serve God with an undivided heart. Because only God can fill our empty hearts.

REFLECTION — *The importance of witness*

Today's Gospel raises very powerfully the importance of witness. Jesus was trying to convince the religious leaders of the truth of his claim that he had been sent by God. He was doing this, not for his own sake, but for their sake. He agreed that his own unsupported testimony to himself need not be true. But he said that there were other witnesses. One of those witnesses was John the Baptist.

John was a powerful witness for Jesus. In the words of Jesus himself, he was 'a lamp alight and shining'. His whole lifestyle, as well as his personal integrity, lent credence to his words. He was a living example of what he preached.

Jesus now depends on us. We are his witnesses before the world. We are meant to be witnesses for the light. We can't be a witness for the light if we are living in darkness. We have to be living in the light. A good life is a strong and effective witness, and in itself is a proclamation of the Gospel. Those who bear witness by their actions are the most valuable witnesses of all.

When religious practice is divorced from one's life a vital element is missing. But when religious practice is expressed in one's life, a very effective witness is given. No witness reaches our contemporaries as persuasively as the witness of those who do what Jesus commanded.

In short, the most effective way to witness to Jesus is to live a Christian life. We can draw inspiration from what Mother Theresa said: 'I don't pray for success; I pray that I may be a faithful witness.'

The task of witnessing is not one for the individual Christian only. It is for the Christian community as a whole. It is easier to witness to Christ as a member of a supportive community.

REFLECTION — *Actions speak louder than words*

During the height of the 'Troubles' in Northern Ireland, a young policeman was driving along a country road when a landmine exploded under his landrover, killing him instantly.

The policeman was a Catholic. When he joined the police force he knew he was putting his life at risk. He claimed he did it in the hope of doing something, however small, to heal the rift between the two communities in the North. Some might not have believed him.

At his funeral a priest revealed that a short time before his death, the young policeman had come to see him. He said that in the event of his getting killed, he wanted all his worldly possessions to go to Mother Theresa of Calcutta. When the people heard this they found it easy to believe the truth of his earlier claim.

Jesus too had a problem in being believed. When we look at today's Gospel, we see that the Jewish leaders did not believe him when he said that he had been sent by God. Since they wouldn't believe his words, he invited them to look at his deeds. He said: 'If my words do not convince you, then let the works I do testify that the Father has sent me.'

There is a well-known saying: Actions speak louder than words. Jesus was quite happy to let his deeds speak for him. Even though those deeds spoke eloquently for him, the religious leaders still refused to believe in him.

We profess to believe that Jesus is the One sent by God. But it is not enough just to believe in him. We have to follow him. We must manifest our faith by the way we live. We are his witnesses before the world. The best witness is that of a Christian life.

Here is a question we might ask ourselves: If it was a crime to be a Christian, and we were put on trial, would there be enough evidence in our lives to secure a conviction?

PRAYER OF THE FAITHFUL

Celebrant: Let us bring our needs before God who sent his

Son to lead us out from sin and death.

Response: Lord, hear our prayer.

Reader(s): For all believers: that they may worship God in spirit and in truth. [Pause] Let us pray to the Lord.

For government leaders: that they may respect freedom of worship for all citizens. [Pause] Let us pray to the Lord.

For those who worship idols: that they may come to know, love and serve the one true God. [Pause] Let us pray to the Lord.

For this congregation: that our lives may bear witness to the faith we profess with our lips. [Pause] Let us pray to the Lord.

For our own special needs. [Longer pause] Let us pray to the Lord.

Celebrant: Father, send your Holy Spirit to make us strong in faith and active in good works, so that we may give you fitting worship. We ask this through Christ our Lord.

PRAYER / REFLECTION

We can't separate our faith from our actions,
or our belief from our occupations.
We can't spread our hours before us, saying,
'This is for God and this is for myself;
this is for my soul and this is for my body.'
Our daily life is our temple and our religion.
Lord, help us to give you the kind of worship
that will honour you and lead others to your kingdom.

FRIDAY OF FOURTH WEEK OF LENT

INTRODUCTION AND CONFITEOR

In this world it seems to be the good who suffer most. But the good know that God is on their side. This gives them peace of mind. Besides, God upholds the just who put their trust in him. [Pause]

Lord Jesus, you are close to the broken-hearted. Lord, have mercy.

You rescue the just from their many trials. Christ, have mercy.

Your save from shame those who take refuge in you. Lord, have mercy.

SCRIPTURE NOTE

Today a note of menace is present in the readings, something that will become more pronounced as we approach Holy Week.

The *First Reading* (Wis 2:1.12-22) tells how the godless plot to do away with the virtuous man because his blameless life is a reproach to them. They plan to test the special relationship he claims to enjoy with God, as well as his powers to stand up under torture.

This passage has been seen in Christian tradition as anticipating the hostility shown to Jesus, the virtuous one *par excellence*. We think of the mockery he had to endure on Calvary (e.g. Mt 27:43). We also have it in today's *Gospel* (Jn 7:1-2.10.25-30), where his life is under threat from the Jewish leaders.

On the feast of Tabernacles (autumn harvest festival) Jesus' disciples wanted him to go up openly to Jerusalem and manifest himself to the world, completely misunderstanding his mission. He did go up, but privately.

In Jerusalem the question that he might be the Messiah was raised. However, there was one obstacle in the way. There was a popular belief that the Messiah's origin would be completely hidden and unknown. The fact that Jesus was known to have come from Nazareth would mean that he could not be the Messiah.

Jesus took up with the crowd the question of his known origin. In one sense his origin was known: he was from Nazareth. But in another sense his origin was not known: he has come from God.

The fact that the Jews cannot recognise Jesus as the one whom the Father sent is evidence that they do not know the Father.

But Jesus does know the Father, because he comes from him and was sent by him. Incensed by what they perceive as the blasphemy of his claim, they sought to arrest him, though no one actually laid hands on him.

REFLECTION — *The suffering of the just*

The First Reading shows how the virtuous person becomes a target for evil people. Good people have always suffered at the hands of the wicked. They suffer because their good and upright lives are a reproach to the wicked, and a judgement on their lives. It is precisely because they are good that they suffer.

Persecution has always been the lot of the righteous. However, it gives them an opportunity to show their true mettle. Besides, the just know that God is on their side. The Credo of the righteous is their unswerving belief in God's love for them. God never abandons the upright, but their reward is in the life-to-come.

As for the evil, even though they may seem to prosper, their punishment is assured even in this world. The anxieties and fears that assail them make their prosperity a bitter one.

Jesus is the virtuous one *par excellence.* Yet he too suffered. Throughout his public ministry he was hounded by his enemies. (Today's Gospel is an example). On the cross he suffered the taunts of his enemies and of the godless.

All those who suffer in the cause of right can draw strength from the example of Jesus. He was victorious, not by avoiding evil, but by confronting it and overcoming it. His death may seem a defeat. It was not a defeat. It was a victory – the victory of good over evil, and of life over death.

Those who travel this road have him as a companion, and will share his victory. To suffer for one's faith, or for doing the right thing, (which for a believer amounts to the same thing), is the way to the closest possible companionship with Jesus.

REFLECTION — *Suffering in the cause of right*

The First Reading tells how the godless plot to do away with the virtuous man because his blameless life has become a reproach to them. This passage has been seen in Christian tradition as anticipating the hostility shown to Jesus, the virtuous one *par excellence*. We have an example in today's Gospel. There we see his life under threat from the Jewish leaders.

It is not easy to remain faithful when evil is in control, and evil people are calling the shots. One feels so alone and so powerless. Yet Jesus says that his disciples should rejoice and count themselves blessed when they suffer in the cause of right: 'Blessed are you when people abuse you, and persecute you, and speak all kinds of calumny against you on my account. Rejoice and be glad, for your reward will be great in heaven; this is how they persecuted the prophets before you' (Matt. 5:10-12).

Why are they blessed? They are blessed because they know their cause is right. The rightness of one's cause gives a person great strength. They are blessed because they are following in the footsteps of the prophets. They draw inspiration from their example. And they are blessed because God is on their side.

And the disciples of Jesus did in fact rejoice when they suffered for preaching the Gospel. We read in the Acts of the Apostles how, after being flogged and warned not to preach in the name of Jesus anymore, 'they left the presence of the Sanhedrin glad to have had the honour of suffering humiliation for the sake of the name' (Acts 5: 40-41).

To suffer for one's faith, or for doing the right thing, (which for a believer amounts to the same thing), is the way to the closest possible companionship with Jesus. Jesus supports all those who follow him down this lonely and difficult road. Anyone who has embarked on this road will not want to turn back.

REFLECTION — *My hour has not yet come*

Some of Jesus' friends urged him to go up to Jerusalem for the feast of Tabernacles. The feast would provide him with a marvellous opportunity to do some great sign and prove to the world that he was the Messiah.

The friends of Jesus were wrong about the Messiah. They saw him as a great popular hero. But this was not Jesus' idea. So he said to them, 'My hour has not yet come.' However, he did eventually go up to the feast privately.

'My hour has not yet come.' This is one of the most telling expressions in John's Gospel. We often talk about somebody's finest hour. We invariably see it as an hour of triumph and glory. This is what the friends of Jesus had in mind for him when they urged him to go up to the feast.

But the hour that Jesus had in mind was the hour of his death. It was an hour in which he made a complete sacrifice of himself for us. He didn't seek his own glory but the glory of God. From a worldly point of view, that hour was an hour of failure. But by raising him from the dead, God turned it into an hour of triumph for Jesus, and an hour of grace for us. This was Jesus' finest hour. All his life had led him to it and prepared him for it.

Paradoxically, our lowest moments can turn out to be our highest and best ones. Moments of great worldly success quickly fade and often leave people empty. On the other hand, moments of darkness, weakness, and failure can prove to be moments of great change and growth. As, for example, when an alcoholic hits rock bottom and, by the grace of God, manages to turn his/her life around.

Looking back at our lives we see that the incidents which seemed to be great failures were the incidents which shaped the lives we have now. Reflecting on what for Jesus was his finest hour will help us to evaluate our lives differently.

PRAYER OF THE FAITHFUL

Celebrant: God listens to the call of the just. Let us call on God now for all our needs.

Response: Lord, hear our prayer.

Reader(s): For Christians who suffer for their beliefs: that God may sustain them. [Pause] Let us pray to the Lord.

For the leaders of governments: that they may defend the weak against the powerful. [Pause] Let us pray to the Lord.

For those who suffer in the struggle for justice. [Pause] Let us pray to the Lord.

For each other and for ourselves: that in our own trials, we may draw strength from the example of the heroes and saints who have gone before us. [Pause] Let us pray to the Lord.

For our own special needs. [Longer pause] Let us pray to the Lord.

Celebrant: All-powerful God, our source of life, you know our weakness. May we reach out with joy to grasp the hand you extend to us in Christ, and so walk more readily in your ways. We make this prayer through the same Christ our Lord.

PRAYER

All those who suffer for their faith,
or for doing the right thing,
can draw strength from the example of Jesus.
Better still: they have him as a companion,
and will share his victory.
He was victorious, not by avoiding evil,
but by confronting it and overcoming it.
His death may have seemed a defeat.
It was not a defeat. It was a victory –
the victory of good over evil,
and of life over death.

SATURDAY OF FOURTH WEEK OF LENT

INTRODUCTION AND CONFITEOR

For Christians, the words of Jesus have an authority no other words have. But it is not enough to listen to his words; we have to do them. We know we haven't always done this, so let us as

God's forgiveness, and the strength to do better in the future.
[Pause]

Lord Jesus, your words are a lamp for our steps. Lord, have mercy.

Your words are the foundation of our lives. Christ, have mercy.

Your words endure for ever. Lord, have mercy.

SCRIPTURE NOTE

The *First Reading* (Jer 11:18-20) gives us an insight into the struggles Jeremiah experienced as he tried to preach God's word in the face of opposition and threats to his life. He did not hesitate to pour out his soul to God, complaining when the Lord seemed to have abandoned him to his enemies. Here he asks God to vindicate him. However, he sees his vindication as involving the downfall of his enemies and prays for vengeance. He was a man of his time and must be judged accordingly. Nevertheless, Christians have always seen him as a figure of Christ.

The *Gospel* (Jn 7:40-53) shows how the crowd (at the feast of Tabernacles) was divided about Jesus. Some said that he was the prophet (who was to precede the Messiah). Others said he was the Messiah himself. A third section argued that he couldn't be the Messiah since he came from Nazareth and not from Bethlehem. (John presupposes that his readers know of the infancy narratives of Matthew and Luke, which establish that Jesus was born in Bethlehem. But the real point he is making is that Jesus did not come in the ultimate sense from Galilee but from the Father).

There was a renewed attempt to arrest him. However, the temple guards were so impressed by his preaching that they refused to arrest him. The reaction of the Pharisees was one of contempt. They and the Scribes despised 'the poor of the land' who had neither the training nor the time to attend to the keeping of the Law in the manner required by authority.

Then Nicodemus (a member of the Sanhedrin) intervened: Jesus should, at least, be given a fair hearing as the law demanded.

But the Pharisees dismiss him on the grounds that Jesus could not be a prophet because he came from Galilee. The whole episode serves to underline the obduracy of Jesus' enemies.

REFLECTION — *The words of Jesus*

The Pharisees sent some of the temple police to arrest Jesus but they came back without him. The reason they gave for not arresting him was: 'No one has ever spoken like this man.'

Teaching was one of the main components of Jesus' ministry. As a teacher he made an immediate impact. Crowds flocked to hear him. His teaching made a deep impression on the people 'because, unlike the Scribes (the official teachers), he taught them with authority.'

His approach was fresh and original. He didn't speak in abstractions. He used concrete images and colourful metaphors. He was able to raise the most profound religious questions through the means of simple things of every day, so that ordinary people were able to understand.

But what most drew people to him was the content of his teaching. Unlike many teachers who are mere providers of facts, he provided vision, inspiration, and meaning. His teaching enlightened the mind, but it also nourished the spirit and set the heart on fire.

The words of the temple police are very revealing in this regard: 'No one has ever spoken like this man.' That statement, coming from people who would not have been particularly disposed in his favour, speaks volumes.

The words of Jesus have echoed down the centuries, bringing light to those in darkness and hope to those in despair. His words continue to illuminate the world. But if his words are to illuminate our lives, it is not enough just to listen to them; we have to do them.

REFLECTION — *Learning from Nicodemus*

Nicodemus, who appears in today's Gospel, is a very interesting character. He was a Pharisee, and a member of the Sanhedrin – the supreme court of the Jews. He is mentioned three times in the Gospel Story, each time by John.

He is first mentioned when he came to see Jesus under cover of darkness. What brought him? He was impressed by the teaching and works of Jesus. It was obvious to him that the hand of God was in them.

The second time he appears is in the Gospel passage we've just read. This was a more public involvement with Jesus. He asked that Jesus be given a fair hearing as the law demanded.

And the third and last time he appears is at the burial of Jesus. It was he who provided a large quantity of expensive spices for his burial.

What can we say about him from these three brief appearances? It's clear that he was *open-minded,* and genuinely searching for the truth. He was also *fair-minded,* insisting that Jesus should not be condemned without a trial. And the last episode shows that he was *a generous and compassionate man.*

All of these qualities we can admire and copy with profit. But what Nicodemus seems to have been unable to do was come straight out and make a full and public act of faith in Jesus.

Reflecting on him should challenges us to come out from the shadows, and not to be afraid or ashamed to profess openly our faith in Jesus, and to be ready to pay whatever price is required for doing so.

REFLECTION — *Opposite views of the same reality*

Two prisoners shared the same prison cell which had only one window onto the outside world. One of them looked out and saw mud. The other looked out and saw stars. Some people see the bad; other people see the good. This is well illustrated in today's Gospel.

Many people observed Jesus. Some saw good in him, others saw evil. Some thought he was the prophet who was to come before the Messiah. Others thought he was the Messiah himself.

But others saw him as a law-breaker and a blasphemer.

How do we account for the fact that people had such radically different views of Jesus? The first set of people listened with open minds to his teaching, looked at his deeds, and concluded that he was good. Among these were the temple guards and Nicodemus.

The second set of people had closed their minds against him from the outset. They did not really know Jesus, and were not prepared to find out. They judged him superficially – by where he came from. Most notable among these were the chief priests and the Pharisees. When Nicodemus invited them to look at the facts and to discern the truth about Jesus, they dismissed him.

If we wish to be fair to people, we must not pre-judge them. The worst kind of blindness of all is that which the Pharisees suffered from – *wilful blindness to the truth.* We should strive to be open-minded, and to give people a chance. Otherwise we may end up like the man in the cell who could see only the mud.

People are still divided over Jesus. Some see him as just a religious teacher, albeit a very great one (as the temple police attested). Others believe he is the Holy One of God who alone has the words of eternal life. Blessed are those who believe.

PRAYER OF THE FAITHFUL

Celebrant: No one ever spoke like Jesus spoke. Let us pray that we may be guided by his teachings.

Response: Lord, hear our prayer.

Reader(s): For Christians: that they may have the courage to profess their faith openly. [Pause] Let us pray to the Lord.

For all who exercise religious or civil authority: that they may be just in their dealings with people. [Pause] Let us pray to the Lord.

For those who are victims of prejudice and discrimination. [Pause] Let us pray to the Lord.

For grace to listen to the words of Jesus, and put them into practice in our lives. [Pause] Let us pray to the Lord.

For our own special needs. [Longer pause] Let us pray to the Lord.

Celebrant: God of truth, deliver us from the cowardice which shrinks from new truth, the laziness that is content with only half the truth, and the arrogance that makes us think we know it all. We ask this through Christ our Lord.

REFLECTION

The Temple police were sent to arrest Jesus.
However, instead of arresting him,
they came back to the Pharisees and declared:
'No one has ever spoken like this man.'
The words of Jesus have echoed down the centuries,
bringing light to those in darkness
and hope to those in despair.
Blessed are those who listen to his words,
and twice blessed are those who do them.

Fifth Week of Lent

MONDAY OF FIFTH WEEK OF LENT

INTRODUCTION AND CONFITEOR

In today's Gospel we hear again the immortal words Jesus spoke to those who wanted him to condemn the woman caught in adultery: 'Let the one who is without sin cast the first stone.' As we call to mind our sins, we might remember especially the harsh judgements we sometimes pass on others. [Pause]

Lord Jesus, you bring pardon and peace to the sinner. Lord, have mercy.

You bind up hearts that are broken. Christ, have mercy.

You bring light to those in darkness and in the shadow of death. Lord, have mercy.

SCRIPTURE NOTE

Susanna (*First Reading*, Dan 13:1-9.15-17.19-30.33-62), a devout and wealthy member of the Jewish community in Babylon, was accused of adultery by two lecherous elders. She was tried and condemned to death on the false evidence of the two elders. However, Daniel defended her by trapping the two elders in contradictory evidence. As a result it was the elders who were executed and Susanna who was spared. The story shows that virtue can triumph over vice. Daniel is portrayed as a hero with God-given wisdom.

The story of Susanna prepares us for the *Gospel* story (Jn 8:1-11). Here we are dealing with a woman who *was* guilty of adultery, yet Jesus refused to condemn her, and saved her life.

The Scribes and Pharisees thought they had set the perfect snare for Jesus. If he pardoned the woman, he could be accused of encouraging people to break the law of Moses. If he agreed that she should be stoned, he would lose his name for mercy. But Jesus turned the tables on her accusers by suggesting that before they condemn her they should look at their own sins.

The lesson of the story is not that sin doesn't matter to God, but that God extends mercy to the sinner so that he/she may turn from sin.

Alternative Gospel, Year C (Jn 8:12-20): Jesus has been sent by the Father, not to condemn the world, but to save it.

REFLECTION — *The story of Susanna*

At first sight the story of Susanna seems more suited to a tabloid newspaper than to the Bible. The story is included in the Bible because in it virtue triumphs over vice. Let us look briefly at some of the characters in the story.

First there is Susanna. Though both rich and beautiful, she didn't allow her beauty to go to her head or her wealth to corrupt her. She was a virtuous, God-fearing woman, who showed great courage.

Next there are the two elders – lustful, corrupt, wretched

figures, who, in Daniel's telling phrase, 'had grown old in wickedness'. It's clear that it wasn't the first time they had done this kind of thing. It was just the first time that someone had the courage to stand up to them. The fact that they were judges made their behaviour all the more reprehensible.

Then there is Daniel. He was that rare person who couldn't stand idly by while an innocent person was being condemned. He felt that if he didn't try to stop it, he would share in the guilt of it. His anger flared up at the great injustice that was being done – it shows that anger has its place and its use. It was thanks to his intervention that justice was done in the end.

It is a very instructive and relevant story. It brings out the beauty of virtue and the ugliness of vice.

The story prepares us for the Gospel story. Here again we see the ugliness of sin. Not just the sin of adultery, but the horrible sin involved in the way the Scribes and Pharisees used the woman as a bait with which to entrap Jesus. But in the end, thanks to the wisdom and compassion of Jesus, good triumphs over evil. The woman was able to put her sin behind her, and all present were taught a salutary lesson.

REFLECTION — *A happy ending*

A scene was being filmed. The leading actor was supposed to drive up in an old car and park it immediately behind a gleaming new Mercedes. However, as he pulled in behind the Merc, his brakes failed and he crashed into it. He jumped out and began to apologise profusely to the director for having ruined the scene. What happened? The director thought the whole scene just wonderful, and wrote it into the script.

That scene could have ended very differently if the director had reacted angrily. Then, when all the recriminations were over, they would have had to go back to the beginning and take the scene again. Instead, thanks to the imagination of the director, they were able to go forward.

The Gospel scene could have ended in a very ugly manner. If

Jesus had gone along with the script of the Scribes and Pharisees, the woman would have died a horrible death, and all present would have gone away diminished. Instead, thanks to the wisdom and compassion of Jesus, the woman was able to put her sin behind her, and all present were taught a salutary lesson.

Jesus, the only sinless one among them, refused to condemn the woman. He distinguished between the sin and the sinner. He condemned the sin but pardoned the sinner.

The story of redemption is a great symphony which embraces all our errors, our bum notes, and in which beauty finally triumphs. It is not that God wipes out our wrong notes, or pretends that they never happened, but that he finds a place for them in the musical score that redeems them.

And surely the fact that we have all sinned, and therefore stand continually in need of God's mercy, will make us refrain from casting stones at others.

REFLECTION — *The radiance of his kindness*

It is hard to underestimate the value of kindness. Kindness is welcome at all times and in all situations. But it is like manna from heaven when one is vulnerable and exposed. In today's Gospel we have a marvellous example of the kindness Jesus showed to one who was in just that kind of situation.

On the surface there appears to be only one sin involved here – the sin of adultery. But there are other sins present. There is the horrible sin involved in the way the Scribes and Pharisees used this woman as a bait with which to entrap Jesus. Then there is the sin involved in their murderous attitude towards Jesus.

Yet, in spite of the way they shamed and humiliated the woman, and the murderous attitudes they harboured towards himself, there is something marvellously gentle and subtle in the way Jesus dealt with them. He didn't condemn them. He didn't even judge them. Instead, he invited them to judge themselves. Reluctantly they were forced to confront their own sinfulness. One by one they slunk away. And Jesus refused to condemn the woman. He said to her, 'Go and sin no more.'

But for Jesus the incident would, in all probability, have ended up with the woman lying as a bleeding mass on the ground. In which case everyone would have gone away diminished. Thankfully it ended very differently. No one died and all were taught a salutary lesson. Jesus illuminated a dark scene with the radiance of his kindness.

The lovely thing about a kindness done to us is that it continues to benefit us long afterwards through the memory we have of it. And the lovely thing about a kindness we do to another is that it benefits us as much as the one for whom we do it. When we treat another person kindly a sweetness falls like dew into our heart.

PRAYER OF THE FAITHFUL

Celebrant: Let us pray for our needs to God who is rich in mercy and compassion.

Response: Lord, hear our prayer.

Reader(s): For Christians: that they may imitate the compassion of Christ in all their dealings with others. [Pause] Let us pray to the Lord.

For lawyers and judges: that they may strive to ensure that justice is done, but also know how to temper justice with mercy. [Pause] Let us pray to the Lord.

For those who have been unfairly treated or unjustly condemned. [Pause] Let us pray to the Lord.

For the victims of sexual assault. [Pause] Let us pray to the Lord.

For grace to extend to others the same compassion we would like to receive if we were in the same situation. [Pause] Let us pray to the Lord.

For our own special needs. [Longer pause] Let us pray to the Lord.

Celebrant: Heavenly Father, help us to keep our hearts pure, our minds clean, our words true, and our deeds kind. We ask this through Christ our Lord.

REFLECTION

The scene in the Gospel was a dark and ugly one.
But Jesus illuminated it with the radiance of his kindness.
The lovely thing about a kindness done to us
is that it continues to benefit us long afterwards,
through the memory we have of it.
And the lovely thing about a kindness we do to another
is that it benefits us as much as the one for whom we do it.
When we treat another person kindly
a sweetness falls like dew into our heart.

TUESDAY OF FIFTH WEEK OF LENT

INTRODUCTION AND CONFITEOR

Three times in today's Gospel Jesus tells the Pharisees that
they will die in their sins. They will die in their sins because they
refuse to acknowledge them. Let us now call to mind our sins,
and ask God for the grace of true repentance. [Pause]

Lord Jesus, you came to reconcile us to one another and to
the Father. Lord, have mercy.

You heal the wounds of sin and division. Christ have mercy.

You intercede for us with the Father. Lord, have mercy.

SCRIPTURE NOTE

In the *First Reading* (Num 21:4-9) we hear how the Israelites
grumble about the hardships of desert life, and question God's
care for them. To compound their difficulties, poisonous snakes
invade their camp and their bites cause many deaths among
them. They interpret this as a direct punishment for the sin of
daring to speak against God and against his prophet. So they
beseech Moses to intercede for them with God. Moses does so,
and is told by God to make a bronze serpent and set it on a pole.

When those who had been bitten look at it, they live. However, it is not the bronze serpent that heals them, but the power of God.

Jesus used this story (*Gospel,* Jn 8:21-30) as a parallel for his saving death on the cross. 'As Moses lifted up the serpent in the wilderness, so must the Son of Man be lifted up, so that whoever believes in him may have eternal life' (Jn 3:14-15). And there is an echo of it in today's Gospel where Jesus talks about being 'lifted up'.

For John the expression 'lifted up' has a double significance when applied to Jesus. It refers to his being raised up on the cross, and to his glorification in the resurrection and ascension to the Father.

Jesus talks about 'going away', a reference to his return to the Father. He confronts the Pharisees with a choice: to believe in him as the one sent from God to bestow the gift of life, or to reject him and so remain in sin. Their obduracy is the sure guarantee that they will die in sin, since they refuse the life that only he can give. After the crucifixion and glorification of Jesus, then – when it is too late – they will perceive the truth about him.

REFLECTION — *Dying in one's sins*

Three times in today's short Gospel passage Jesus tells the Pharisees that they will die in their sins. Their greatest sin was their stubborn refusal to believe in him, the One sent by the Father to save us from our sins.

Klaus Barbie, known as the Butcher of Lyon, died there on September 25, 1991, at the age of 77. After the war, Barbie, the Gestapo boss of Lyon, evaded justice for nearly four decades. But he was eventually tracked down, tried, and sentenced to life imprisonment for crimes against humanity.

Among the crimes he was convicted of was the torture and killing of Jean Moulin, the great hero of the French Resistance. He was also charged with the arrest of 44 Jewish orphans, whom he had transported to Germany where they died in a concentration camp.

Barbie remained defiant to the end. When a reporter asked him if he regretted what he had done he answered, 'What is there to regret? I am proud of having been a commanding officer of the best military outfit in the Third Reich.' Here surely was a man who died in his sins.

The prospect of dying in one's sins is a terrifying one. All of us are to a greater or lesser extent drawn towards evil, and once we succumb, it is hard to break free. Each time we repeat that choice it becomes more of a habit, to the point where it eventually becomes part of our character.

Every evil act tends to harden a person's heart. The more a person's heart hardens, the less freedom there is to change. But the opposite is also true. Every good deed tends to soften a person's heart. Every time we do something good, we make it easier to do good again.

Jesus came not to condemn us but to save us. In order to be saved, we have to confess our sins. But this is seldom easy. Pride makes it difficult for us to confess. However, if we do confess our sins, we have nothing to fear but the mercy of God.

REFLECTION — *Healing the wounds of sin*

The Israelites found life in the desert very hard. So they grumbled against Moses and against God. God sent poisonous snakes into their camp. The bite of the snakes caused many deaths among them.

Taken literally, the story portrays God as an angry, jealous God, who will resort to the most terrible punishments when his law is disobeyed.

But we can look at the story another way. The Israelites grumbled about the hardships of desert life, and questioned God's care for them. To compound matters, poisonous snakes invaded their camp and their bites caused many deaths among them. They interpreted this as a direct punishment for the sin of daring to speak against God and against his prophet.

Let's be clear about this. God was not responsible for the snakes or for the deaths that occurred among the Israelites. God doesn't hurt his people. God cares for his people. We see how, in response to the prayer of Moses, God took pity on them and healed their wounds. It was not the bronze serpent that healed them; it was the power of God.

We are not punished *for* our sins; we are punished *by* our sins. Sin brings its own punishment. Just as the poison of snakebite can cause physical death, so the poison of sin can cause spiritual death.

The Israelites could do nothing to heal the wounds of the serpents. But God gave them a simple remedy. All they had to do was acknowledge their sins and look at the bronze snake. Of course, it was not a question of merely looking, repentance was needed.

In the same way we can do nothing to heal the wounds of sin. But God has given us a simple remedy. We need only admit our sins and look at the crucified Christ with faith and repentance. Then we will never know the death that is the penalty of sin, but will have eternal life.

REFLECTION — *The price of freedom*

The Israelites left the slavery of Egypt in joy, and set off into what they believed would be a bright future. But things didn't turn out as they imagined. They found themselves in the desert, having to contend with heat and cold, with hunger and thirst.

Thus they soon discovered that freedom presented its own challenges. Freedom meant taking responsibility for their own lives. It meant learning to master themselves and their passions. It called for self-discipline. It is easier to be disciplined by others than to discipline oneself.

But rather than look at themselves they turned on Moses. They grumbled about the hardships of desert life, and questioned God's care for them. To compound matters, poisonous snakes invaded their camp and their bites caused many deaths among them. They interpreted this as a direct punishment for the sin of daring to speak against God and against his prophet.

God was not responsible for the snakes or for the deaths that occurred among the Israelites. God doesn't hurt his people. God cares for his people. In response to the prayer of Moses, God took pity on them and healed their wounds. It was not the bronze serpent that healed them, but the power of God.

We are the new People of God, journeying in faith towards the promised land of eternal life. By our baptism we have been called out of slavery to sin into the freedom of the children of God. We are led, not by Moses, but by Jesus.

And we are bound to experience the desert of trial and difficulty. But just as God sustained the Israelites, so God sustains us through faith in Jesus. No matter how difficult life may be, for those who trust in God, and live a day at a time, the manna of his help falls every day.

PRAYER OF THE FAITHFUL

Celebrant: God heard the cry of his people in their distress. Let us pray to him with confidence for all our needs.

Response: Lord, graciously hear us.

Reader(s): For the Church: that through its ministry of reconciliation, sinners may experience the tender mercy of God. [Pause] Lord, hear us.

For those who are on a wrong path: that they may come out of the darkness and walk in the light of truth and goodness. [Pause] Lord, hear us.

For the grace of true repentance. [Pause] Lord, hear us.

For healing for the wounds caused by our own sins and the sins of others. [Pause] Lord, hear us.

For our own special needs. [Longer pause] Lord, hear us.

Celebrant: Heavenly Father, you sent your Son into the world to forgive our sins and heal our wounds. Help us to have complete faith in his healing power and in your love for us. We ask this through the same Christ our Lord.

PRAYER

Lord Jesus, you took our sins on yourself,
and were wounded for them on the cross.
Help us to so to look at your wounds
that we may find forgiveness and healing.
And when at times we stray like sheep,
take pity on us and bring us back to yourself,
the Shepherd and Guardian of our souls.

WEDNESDAY OF FIFTH WEEK OF LENT

INTRODUCTION AND CONFITEOR

In the Bible sin is seen as a manifestation of slavery. Let us call to mind our sins, and ask the Lord to set us free of them. When the Lord sets us free, we are free indeed. [Pause]

Lord Jesus, you guide the humble in the right path. Lord, have mercy.

You show the path to those who stray. Christ, have mercy.

You reveal the truth that sets us free. Lord, have mercy.

SCRIPTURE NOTE

The *First Reading* (Dan 3:14-20.91-92.95) tells how three young Israelites (Shadrach, Meshach, and Abednego) were thrown into a fiery furnace by king Nebuchadnezzar because they refused to worship an idol – a golden statue of his pagan god. The three affirm God's ability to save them, but assert that even if God doesn't save them, they will still refuse to worship an idol. The story emphasises God's power and his protection of those who are faithful to him.

The *Gospel* (Jn 8:31-42) tells us that at the end of the discourse in the Temple some Jews believed in Jesus. Jesus told these that merely to be receptive of his word is not enough; they must take it in and act on it constantly. Then they will come to know the truth, and the truth will make them free. For Jesus sin is a manifestation of a state of slavery. But he can set people free.

The greatest claim of the Jews was that they were descended from Abraham. Jesus now passes from the description of the Jews as slaves of sin in their rejection of him to a direct challenge to their claim to be true children of Abraham. He begins by admitting their claim to physical descent from Abraham. But spiritually they are not his children.

If they were his children they would do as he did; he welcomed three messengers of God, even though they were 'incognito' (Gen. 18). Unlike Abraham they not only reject God's messenger (Jesus), but actually seek to kill him. They are doing what their father (the devil) does. This is tantamount to a charge of spiritual illegitimacy, and the Jews quickly reject it. But Jesus insists that if God was their father they would accept himself since he was sent by the Father.

REFLECTION — *The truth will set you free*

In trying to convince the Jews that he was sent by God, Jesus invited them to open themselves to the truth. He assured them that if they did, the truth would set them free.

'The truth will set you free.' This is one of most frequently-quoted sayings of the Gospel. It is hard to underestimate the value of truth. Truth brings clarity and simplicity to life. It liberates us from the darkness of error and from the entanglements of lies and deceit. Truth is a straight path. Truth is a bright path. Yet how hard it is to find a person who is totally open to the truth.

The enemies of truth are ignorance, denial, deception, lies. To walk in ignorance and denial is to walk in darkness. To walk in deception is to walk a slippery path. To walk in lies is to walk a crooked path.

Sometimes the truth is not so obvious, so we have to search for it. Other times it is staring us in the face. It's just that we don't have the courage to face it. It can take great courage to face the truth. But those who do will experience the truth of Jesus' words: the truth will set them free. We are God's children, made to delight in the truth.

Sometimes it is our duty to speak the truth to someone who is in error. To do this effectively we have to do it with love and concern for the person. It goes without saying that we can't guide another if we are in darkness ourselves.

If we want to be disciples of Jesus we must strive to live by the truth of the Gospel. Jesus says that we must 'make his word (his teaching) our home'. God has revealed himself to us in Jesus. To walk in his truth is to walk in the light. It is to be free.

REFLECTION — *Sustained by God*

The First Reading tells how three young Israelites were thrown into a fiery furnace by king Nebuchadnezzar because they refused to worship an idol. The story is one of cruelty and barbarity. But it doesn't have to be taken literally.

The story can be seen as a parable. The furnace stands for the crucible which the just sometimes have to suffer. It can take many forms.

To say that those three young Israelites were in a desperate situation would be an understatement. Still, they had two things going for them.

Firstly, they were three of them. That means they were able to support one another. In a time of crisis support it vital.

Secondly, and more importantly, they had God's support. When Nebuchadnezzar looked into the furnace, he was amazed to see that there were not three but four people inside it. This is a way of saying that God was with them in the furnace.

The story shows the depth of the commitment of the three young Israelites to their faith. It also shows the strength they derived from their faith in God.

Faith is our greatest ally in a time of crisis. What faith does is assure us that God is with us *in the midst of the crisis*. It is this conviction which enables us to get through the crisis.

Many Christians have gone bravely to their deaths rather than bow down before the powers of this world. They had faith that God was with them even if he did not miraculously preserve them as he did the three young men.

Jesus himself went through the fiery furnace of his passion and death. Even though he died to this life, by the power of God he emerged triumphant through his resurrection.

REFLECTION — *Abraham, model of faith*

Abraham is mentioned five times in today's Gospel. He is the great biblical model of faith. At the word of God he left everything – home, family, country – and set out for a land he had never seen. The only compass he had was faith in God's promise. God rewarded his faith by making him the father of a great people. It was from his descendants that Christ came.

The Jews prided themselves on being the descendants of Abraham. As such they believed they had a right to inherit the promise God made to him. But Jesus told them they would have to prove themselves true children of Abraham by imitating his faith. The faith that was being asked of them was faith in Jesus as sent by God. Sadly, they failed to imitate the faith of Abraham.

Faith is not something that can be inherited like a possession. Each of us must make it our own. Our faith is bound to be put to the test. Even though we may never have to enter the fiery furnace, we may have to cope with a situation which, from a human point of view, seems impossible. It is then that we discover whether or not we have any faith at all.

It is impossible to over emphasise the value of faith in a time of crisis. It was faith that sustained the three young Israelites during their ordeal. Faith assured them that God was with them in the midst of the crisis. Blessed are we if we have even a grain of real faith.

As Christians we are journeying in faith to the promised land of eternal life. We must not see ourselves as journeying alone.

We journey as members of a believing community. The faith of the community supports us when our own faith does not measure up.

PRAYER OF THE FAITHFUL

Celebrant: The Lord rescues us from all our distress. Let us pray to him with great faith.

Response: Lord, hear our prayer.

Reader(s): For all Christians: that they may walk in the light of truth and goodness. [Pause] Let us pray to the Lord.

For political and civil leaders: that they may strive to create a society in which people can enjoy religious freedom, security, and peace. [Pause] Let us pray to the Lord.

For those who are suffering because of their faith in Christ. [Pause] Let us pray to the Lord.

For all gathered here: that our faith in God may give us strength when we are weak, and courage when we are afraid. [Pause] Let us pray to the Lord.

For our own special needs. [Longer pause] Lord, hear us.

Celebrant: God our Father, you are the same yesterday, today, and forever; help us to have confidence in your unchanging love for us, so that when things are difficult we may persevere in goodness. We ask this through Christ Our Lord.

REFLECTION

Sometimes there is nothing we can do for the person
who is suffering, and nothing we can say either.
Our only ministry is that of simple presence.
The ministry of simple presence is not an easy one.
It is a ministry of powerlessness
like that of Mary at the foot of the cross.
Yet, just by being there,
we save the sufferer from feeling abandoned,
and offer something very precious, namely, human comfort.

THURSDAY OF FIFTH WEEK OF LENT

INTRODUCTION AND CONFITEOR

We are not just God's people; we are God's family. Whereas God is always faithful to us, sadly, we are not always faithful to God. Let us call to mind our infidelities. [Pause]

Lord Jesus, you are faithful in all your words and loving in all your deeds. Lord, have mercy.

You support all who fall, and raise up all who are bowed down. Christ, have mercy.

You are close to all who call on you, who call on you from their hearts. Lord, have mercy.

SCRIPTURE NOTE

The *First Reading* (Gen 17:3-9) deals with the solemn covenant which God made with Abraham. This covenant led to the covenant at Sinai, and culminated in the new and eternal covenant which Jesus sealed in his own blood on Calvary. The Old Testament is a chronicle of the repeated failures of the chosen people to keep their side of the covenant.

In the *Gospel* (Jn 8:51-59)1 Jesus says to the Jews: 'Whoever keeps my word [accepts my teaching] will never see death.' Never to see death is not never to undergo bodily death; it is rather not to undergo the death of the soul. However, the Jews interpret it as referring to the former, and protest against his claim. Is he greater than Abraham and the prophets, all of whom are dead?

Jesus answers that the truth of what he has said depends, not on his own claim, but on the testimony of the Father, the testimony they refuse to receive. They do not know the Father. But he knows him and keeps his word.

Abraham was shown the age to come, that is, the days of the Messiah. He rejoiced at the disclosure of a future blessing for himself and all the peoples of the world (First Reading). 'Before Abraham was, I am' is one of Jesus' most emphatic affirmations of his divinity. This was not lost on the Jews, who sought to stone him for his supposed blasphemy.

REFLECTION — *The covenant*

'Covenant' is not a word we use very often. We are more familiar with the word 'contract'. There is a big difference between a contract and a covenant. A contract is a strictly business arrangement. A covenant is based on love and friendship.

'Covenant' is a key word in the Bible. It is used to described God's relationship with his people. God didn't make a contract with his people; he made a covenant with them. The First Reading tells of the solemn covenant God made with Abraham. After the story of creation, this is the key moment in the Old Testament.

It was not Abraham who took the initiative in establishing this covenant. It was God. God promised Abraham numerous descendants. He promised that his descendants would have a land of their own. And he promised that through him all the nations of the earth would be blessed because the Messiah would come from his line.

God's promise to Abraham was fulfilled in Jesus. It is through him, the Messiah, that all the nations of the earth are blessed. He sealed the covenant anew in his own blood. Through him we have a closer bond than ever with God. We are not just God's people; we are God's family.

Even though the people repeatedly broke God's covenant, God never abandoned them. In and through his Son, God has bound himself to us by a bond that can never be broken. God's steadfast love for us enjoins on us a reciprocal obligation to God and to one another.

Jesus is the head of the new People of God. The land to which he leads us is not some piece of earthly land, but the land of eternal life.

It would be appropriate to use Eucharistic Prayer for
Reconciliation I with its Preface.

REFLECTION — *Keeping his word*

Jesus said to the Jews: 'Whoever keeps my word will never see death.' It is a wonderful promise. However, never to see death is not never to undergo bodily death; it is rather not to undergo the death of the soul.

What does keeping his word mean? It means accepting his teaching. It involves Christian discipleship. We can't truly call ourselves disciples of Jesus if we don't listen to his words and make an effort to live by them. One wouldn't be much of a Christian if one didn't try to live as Jesus taught.

There are those who proclaim their love for Jesus in words, but who deny him in their deeds. Real love is shown in deeds. People know us by our acts, not by what we say with our lips. It is through obedience to his word that we show our love for Jesus. To love is to obey. And to obey is to love.

It's not easy to live as a disciple of Jesus in the modern world. The challenge facing Christians is indifference rather than hostility. Our struggle is not against persecution; it is more subtle, and therefore more insidious. We face being ignored.

It never was easy to be a disciple of Jesus. But for that reason Jesus has given us the Holy Spirit. The Spirit comforts us in times of sorrow, enlightens us in times of darkness, and makes us brave and strong in times of difficulty.

REFLECTION — *The promised land*

A couple booked a passage on a ship they thought was going to an off-shore island which they longed to visit. They set out believing they were bound for an exciting destination. However, they weren't long out at sea when they discovered that the ship wasn't going there after all. It was a cruise ship with a casino on board, and was just going out to sea for the day.

For them the trip was suddenly robbed of expectation, and plundered of meaning. The fact that the day was fine, the sea calm, and they had everything on board by way of food and entertainment they could possibly desire, was of little consolation to them. As far as they was concerned they were on a voyage to nowhere.

God promised a homeland to Abraham. But Jesus gave a new and wonderful dimension to this promise. He said, 'If anyone keeps my word he will never taste death.' Obviously he wasn't talking about physical death but rather the death of the soul. To keep his word is to live by his teaching.

Those who believe in Jesus and who follow him, enter into a relationship with God which death cannot end. They go, not from life to death, but from life on earth to life in the kingdom of heaven. Heaven is our true homeland.

Without the hope of arriving one day at such a land, the voyage of life, no matter how pleasurable it might be, would be robbed of ultimate meaning. In essence, it would be a voyage to nowhere. But our faith assures us that the voyage of life is bound for a wonderful destination. It is bound for the promised land of eternal life. The very hardships and difficulties we encounter on route will add to the joy of arrival.

PRAYER OF THE FAITHFUL

Celebrant: In and through his Son, God has bound himself to us in an everlasting covenant of love. Let us pray to him to strengthen the bonds that bind us to him and to one another.

Response: Lord, hear us in your love.

Reader(s): For members of the Church, the new people of God: that God's word may take root in their hearts and bear fruit in their lives. [Pause] Let us pray in faith.

For political leaders: that God may guide them in their search for justice and peace. [Pause] Let us pray in faith.

For refugees, and all those without a homeland. [Pause] Let us pray in faith.

For grace to be conscious of belonging to a community, and to see our destiny as linked to that of our brothers and sisters. [Pause] Let us pray in faith.

For our own special needs. [Longer pause] Let us pray in

faith.

Celebrant: Father, give us a love for what you command and a longing for what you promise, so that amid this world's changes, our hearts may be set on the world of lasting joy. We make this prayer through Christ our Lord.

PRAYER

Heavenly Father, in and through your Son, you have bound yourself to us in an everlasting covenant of love.

Give us the grace to rise above our human weakness,

and keep us faithful to you and to one another,

as we journey towards the promised land of eternal life.

We ask this through Christ our Lord.

FRIDAY OF FIFTH WEEK OF LENT

INTRODUCTION AND CONFITEOR

All of us experience difficult times. We can draw comfort from the fact that all the saints and prophets knew difficult times. It is at such times that we realise how much we need God's help. Let us turn to God now for strength in our difficulties. [Pause]

Lord Jesus, you are close to the broken-hearted. Lord, have mercy.

You rescue the just from their many trials. Christ, have mercy.

You save from shame those who take refuge in you. Lord, have mercy.

SCRIPTURE NOTE

Jeremiah's cry (*First Reading,* Jer 20:10-13) 'terror on every side' (see 20:3) is now turned against him in derision and mockery. People who once were his friends have now turned against him, hoping to see his downfall so that they can take their revenge on him. Jeremiah, however, keeps faith in God, confident that God will vindicate him.

However, he sees his vindication as involving the downfall of his enemies and prays for vengeance. In this respect he was a man of his time and must be judged accordingly. Nevertheless, Christians have always seen him as a figure of Christ.

In the *Gospel* (Jn 10:31-42) the Jews accuse Jesus of blasphemy and want to stone him because he claims to be God. Jesus replies to the charge by appealing to the Scriptures (quoting Ps. 82:6). He argues that if Scripture sometimes speaks of mere men as 'gods', then he is not necessarily blaspheming when he applies that title to himself.

He then appeals once more to the witness of his works. These, which are of divine origin, justify his claim. The Jews are not convinced and make a further attempt to arrest him but he eludes them. He goes to the far side of the Jordan where John the Baptist had first borne witness to him, a witness that has proved to be true.

This incident brings to an end the long section in which John has outlined the swiftly developing crisis between Jesus and the Jews. He has made it clear that the conflict was about a final theological judgement that people have to pass on Jesus: Is he, or is he not, the Son of the Father, sent by him into the world for its salvation?

REFLECTION — *Going on in spite of everything*

It is a good idea to take a breather at vital moments in life. It gives us a chance to assess how things are going, to correct what needs to be corrected, and to rededicate ourselves to the chosen road.

After eluding those who wanted to arrest him, Jesus went to the far side of the Jordan. He was not running away. He was taking a breather. And he was also gathering strength for the ordeal that lay ahead.

It gave him an opportunity to look back. This was the place his public ministry had begun. Here he made his first public appearance. Here he was baptised by John. Here John bore witness to him. Here he met his first disciples. It was like going back to where he received his vocation.

It also gave him an opportunity to look ahead. The Passover was coming. It would take him to Jerusalem, where the official attitude was deeply hostile to him. He knew he was going into the lion's den.

It would have been a good moment to quit. However, he had said to his disciples, 'No one who puts his hand to the plough and then looks back is fit for the Kingdom of heaven.' He would give an example of what he meant by this. He would not turn back. He had grown into his vocation and would not opt out now. He would remain faithful to the mission given him by his Father.

Jesus gives us an example of faithfulness in a time of darkness. To be faithful in a time of darkness is to be doubly faithful.

REFLECTION — *Faithfulness*

Jeremiah was called to be a prophet from an early age. He lived out his vocation during a time of great turmoil which saw the defeat of Israel and the destruction of Jerusalem and the Temple. He sacrificed everything, including marriage, for his vocation. He indicted the official leaders for neglecting their duties towards the people, blaming them for the misfortune that had befallen the people. He lived with constant threats to his life.

Yet it seemed that his mission had failed. In our First Reading we see him surrounded by terror. Even his friends have turned against him. Nevertheless, he commits his cause to God, confident that God will vindicate him. However, he sees his vindication as involving the downfall of his enemies and prays for vengeance. He was a man of his time and must be judged accordingly. We, the followers of Jesus, have not been spectacularly faithful to the Master's revolutionary call that we pray for our enemies and persecutors.

Christians have always seen Jeremiah as a figure of Christ. He loved his people dearly and never lost faith in the power of God to save them. His sufferings prefigure the sufferings of Jesus. And, in spite of everything, he remained faithful to his vocation.

Jeremiah's faithfulness prefigures the faithfulness of Jesus. Even as the opposition mounted, and the threats to his life increased, Jesus remained faithful to the mission the Father had given him. In today's Gospel we see how he eluded his enemies, and went to the far side of the Jordan. He was not running away. He was gathering his strength for the ordeal that lay ahead.

Jesus gives us an example of faithfulness in a time of darkness. With his example to inspire us, and his grace to strengthen us, we too can be faithful to our vocation as his disciples.

REFLECTION — *The witness of his works*

The Jewish leaders refused to believe Jesus when he said that he had been sent by God. Since they refused to believe his words, he appealed to the witness of the works he was doing in the Father's name. He even went so far as to say that if he was not doing his Father's work, then there was no need for them to believe me. But if he was doing his Father's work, then they ought to believe him on the strength of that work.

This reminds us of what he said on another occasion. He told his disciples that the way to tell a true prophet from a false one was to look at his deeds. Just as you can tell a good tree from a bad one by the quality of the fruit it produces, so you can tell a genuine prophet from a false one by the kind of deeds they do.

The Jewish leaders saw the many good deeds that Jesus had done, yet they refused to believe in him. The evidence that he was genuine was staring them in the face, yet they refused to accept it. They have closed their minds and hardened their hearts against him. Instead of believing in him, they made a further attempt to arrest him, but he eluded them.

Jesus was able to appeal to the testimony of his works. Those works bore eloquent witness to the truth of his claim that he had been sent by God. We profess to be disciples of Jesus. Do our deeds bear witness to the faith we profess with our lips?

We must strive to ensure that our deeds match our profession of faith. Our deeds ought to be such as to bring glory to God, and enable others to find their way into the Kingdom.

PRAYER OF THE FAITHFUL

Celebrant: God is close to all who call on him from their hearts. Let us call on him now in our many needs.

Response: Lord, graciously hear us.

Reader(s): For Christians: that they may be faithful witnesses for Christ in an indifferent and sometimes hostile world. [Pause] Lord, hear us.

For all who hold public office: that they may carry out their responsibilities faithfully. [Pause] Lord, hear us.

For all those who are suffering because of their faith in Christ. [Pause] Lord, hear us.

For all in this congregation: that our deeds may bear witness to the faith we profess with our lips. [Pause] Lord, hear us.

For our own special needs. [Longer pause] Lord, hear us.

Celebrant: Lord, grant us in all our tasks your help, in all our doubts your guidance, in all our weaknesses your strength, in all our dangers your protection, and in all our sorrows your consolation. We ask this through Christ our Lord.

REFLECTION

Blessed are the faithful – they will be like safe anchors
in a world of broken moorings.
Blessed are the caring – they will shine out like beacons
in a world darkened by indifference.
Blessed are the genuine – they will glow like gems
in a world of falseness.
Blessed are those who are not afraid of sacrifice –
on the day of the harvest they will sing for joy
And blessed are those who refuse to look back –

they will be found worthy of the Kingdom of Heaven.

SATURDAY OF FIFTH WEEK OF LENT

INTRODUCTION AND CONFITEOR

God sent his Son into the world to gather together his scattered children. Through his death and resurrection, Jesus gathers together God's scattered flock. Let us open ourselves to the love of Jesus, the Good Shepherd. [Pause]

Lord Jesus, you heal the wounds of sin and division. Lord, have mercy.

You reconcile us to one another and to the Father. Christ, have mercy.

You gather the nations into the peace of God's kingdom. Lord, have mercy.

SCRIPTURE NOTE

The *First Reading* (Ezek 37:2-28) looks forward to a golden age when God will gather together his scattered people, and re-establish his covenant with them under a new 'David'. Jesus is the new 'David', who by his death unites the scattered children of God.

The great sign that Jesus had done (the raising of Lazarus) caused defections from the Jewish faith to him (*Gospel*, Jn 11:45-56). Fearing that he was becoming so popular with the people that the Romans would intervene and destroy the Temple and the Jewish nation, the religious leaders called a meeting of the Sanhedrin (the supreme court of the Jews) to decide what to do about him.

Caiphas suggested that it was better one person should die rather than that the whole nation should perish. Without realising it, what he said was prophetic: Jesus would indeed die for the nation, and thereby gather together God's scattered people, Jew and Gentile alike.

As a result of their determination to kill him, Jesus withdrew to the edge of the desert. He was not running away. He was preparing himself for the final confrontation with the authorities which would happen at the feast of the Passover.

REFLECTIONS — *One must die*

Once an axe needed a handle, so it went into the forest in search of a piece of wood. It looked at the giant pines and great oaks. 'No, don't take us,' they said in a chorus. 'Take that sapling over there. That will make a nice handle for you, and the forest won't miss it.'

So the axe attacked the little sapling. No voice was raised in its defence. When the axe had fitted itself with a handle from the sapling, what did it do? Straightaway it laid siege to the pines and oaks, and felled them one by one. The latter now bitterly regretted having betrayed their little brother. 'If only we had stuck together,' they lamented, 'we would have prevented the axe from harming any of us.'

The chief priests and Pharisees held a meeting to decide what to do with Jesus. It's clear that they had already made up their minds to kill him. At that meeting no voice was raised on his behalf. Instead, the great and authoritative voice of Caiphas the high priest declared, 'It is better that one man should die rather than that a whole nation should perish.'

There was a certain logic in his suggestion. But it was wrong in essence because it involved the killing of an innocent man. Doom was indeed hanging over Jerusalem. But in killing Jesus they killed the person who more than anyone else wanted to prevent it, and could have done so had they listened to him.

Caiphas made sure that the one to die would not be himself or any of his cronies. It's easy to let someone else take the rap while excusing oneself. The death of even one innocent person is wrong no matter what authority sanctions it.

Good would indeed come from the death of Jesus, a good so great that Caiphas could never have envisaged it. The death of

Jesus would bring salvation to all those who believed in him. He would gather together God's scattered people, Jew and Gentile alike.

REFLECTIONS — *Gathering God's scattered children*

During the Second World War Holland was occupied by Germany. As the crematoria and gas chambers were rising in the East, Dutch Jews were rounded up and interrogated. They were forced to wear a yellow star in public.

Dutch Christians responded to these indignities by treating the Jews with emphatic respect. In a marvellous display of solidarity with their Jewish brethren, some of them decided to wear a yellow star themselves. Before such courage one feels poor.

As a result of the raising of Lazarus many Jews believed in Jesus. Fearing that he was becoming so popular with the people that the Romans would intervene and destroy the Temple and the Jewish nation, the religious leaders called a meeting of the Sanhedrin (the supreme court of the Jews) to decide what to do about him.

Caiphas, the high priest, suggested that it was better one person should die rather than that the whole nation should perish. There was a certain logic in his suggestion. But it was wrong in essence because it involved the killing of an innocent man. And it seems that no one had the courage to speak up in defence of Jesus.

Nevertheless, without realising it, what Caiphas said was prophetic. Jesus died suspended between heaven and earth, with arms outstretched so as to gather together the children of God, dispersed by sin, and set against each other, and against God himself.

It is the mission of the Church to gather together the scattered children of God. The Church accomplishes this when it is present where there is conflict and division as a unifying and reconciling force. Even though religion has often been the cause of conflict and division, nevertheless, the Gospel has a great capacity to break down barriers. Of all the things which draw people together, worship alone has the power to turn them into a loving family.

REFLECTION — *United by his death*

A man who lived in a small Irish town died suddenly in a tragic accident. Word went out at once to a son in England, a daughter in Germany, another daughter in America, and a son in Australia. By the time the day of the funeral arrived his scattered family had been gathered together – the first time in many years.

The community was gathered together too. Practically every person in the town turned up for the funeral. To see this vast throng walk through the town after the hearse was a deeply moving sight. It was a wonderful tribute to the deceased man and a marvellous display of solidarity with his family.

Nothing brings people together the way death does, especially the tragic death of a good person. It not only brings the community out in numbers, but unites it in such a way that it speaks, acts, and feels as one. Things that normally divide people are swept away on the day of death life chaff in the wind.

The death of Jesus was not a tragic accident. It was planned in a cold and calculating way by the chief priests and Pharisees. Despite their attempts to justify it, it was a foul deed. Yet God brought great good out of it. Jesus died not just for the Jewish nation, but to gather together God's scattered children, Jews and Gentiles alike.

When we look a little deeper we realise that it is not death which unites people but love. It's just that it takes something like death to enable people to reach out to one another. In the death of Jesus we see God's wonderful love for us, and we are drawn towards him and one another. Love is the greatest unifying force of all. We are saved not by Jesus' suffering but by his love

PRAYER OF THE FAITHFUL

Celebrant: Jesus died to gather together God's scattered children. Let us pray that this unity may become a reality in the Church and in the world.

Response: Lord, hear us in your love.

Reader(s): For unity among all the followers of Christ. [Pause] We pray in faith.

For all the nations of the world: that they may realise that they are one family under God. [Pause] We pray in faith.

For those who have been the victims of injustice. [Pause] We pray in faith.

For grace to show solidarity with those who are unfairly treated. [Pause] We pray in faith.

For our own special needs. [Longer pause] We pray in faith.

Celebrant: Lord our God, you so loved the world that you gave your Son up to death for our sake. Strengthen us by your grace so that we may be willing to live by that same love. We ask this through Christ our lord.

PRAYER

Heavenly Father, through the Gospel proclaimed by your Son,
you have brought together in a single Church
people of every nation, culture, and tongue.
Renew the Church in our times,
so that in a world torn by conflict and division,
it may stand forth as a sign of unity
and an instrument of your peace.
We ask this through Christ our Lord.

Holy Week

MONDAY OF HOLY WEEK

INTRODUCTION AND CONFITEOR

We have entered the holiest week in the Church's year. During this week our attention is focussed on the Passion of Jesus. There is a note of desperation in the liturgy. In desperate times God is our only hope. Let us turn to the Lord now. [Pause]

Lord Jesus, you are our light and our help. Lord, have mercy. You are the stronghold of our lives. Christ, have mercy.

Though father and mother forsake us, you will receive us. Lord, have mercy.

SCRIPTURE NOTE

During Holy Week, pride of place among the Old Testament readings goes to the four 'Songs of the Servant of Yahweh' which are contained in Second Isaiah. The first (42:1-7) is read on Monday, the second (49:1-6) on Tuesday, the third (50:4-9) on Palm Sunday and Wednesday, and the fourth (52:13-53:12), the most famous of them all, on Good Friday. These depict a perfect servant of Yahweh, who preaches the true faith, expiates the people's sins by his own death, and is glorified by God. The New Testament writers saw these songs as being perfectly fulfilled in Jesus.

Today's *First Reading* (Is 42:1-7) contains the first of the Servant Songs. God upholds his chosen servant in whom he delights and whom he has filled with his spirit. (These words are applied to Jesus at his baptism in Mark 1:11 and transfiguration in Matthew 17:5). He will go about his mission quietly and gently. (This is applied to Jesus in Matthew 12:20). His mission is to establish true justice on earth. He will bring relief to the afflicted and liberation to the oppressed. (Jesus applied this to himself in the synagogue at Nazareth: Luke 4:18-21)

The *Gospel* (Jn 12: 1-11) tells the story of the anointing of

Jesus during a banquet given in his honour by Martha and Mary. John uses the story as a foretelling of Jesus' death.

In accordance with the portrait Luke has given of them (10:38-42), Martha is serving at table while Mary devotes herself to the Lord. The anointing with nard (an expensive, fragrant oil), a simple act of devotion and gratitude, took on the added significance of anointing his body for burial. Her act is criticised by Judas on the grounds that the money spent on the ointment would have been better spent on the poor. There is a place for service to the poor; but there must also be a place for expressing our love for our friends.

REFLECTION — *Deeds of the heart*

Sometimes a small act of kindness can take on great significance. Donald Nicholl (an English Catholic and academic) told of an incident which happened to him at Heathrow airport. It was early in the morning and the place was almost deserted. He had just come from the bedside of his dying father, and was feeling sad and forlorn.

He looked around in vain for the place where he was supposed to wait for a stand-by seat on a flight to San Francisco. Then a woman in a uniform came around the corner. He approached her and asked for directions. 'Come with me, my love,' she said. Having taken him to the correct check-in desk, she left him, saying, 'There you are. Have a safe journey.'

It was only a small deed, yet he said that his numbed heart was melted by the warmth in her voice as she said the words, 'Come with me, my love'.

Deeds don't have to be big in order to be of help and comfort to the person for whom they are done. They just have to have a certain quality. That quality is *warmth*. All deeds which come from the heart have this quality.

In spite of the amount of expensive ointment Mary used, her gesture of anointing the feet of Jesus was in itself a small one. But it was a gesture that came from her heart. This is the reason why it went straight to the heart of Jesus.

Surrounded by people who always wanted things from him, and by the hostility of those who were plotting his death, it was as welcome as a cold drink on a hot day. Moreover, it took on an added significance. Unwittingly Mary had anointed his body for burial.

Few of us get the chance to perform great deeds. But every day we get the chance to perform small deeds. Small deeds may not look much, but they can bring peace. It is not how much we do that matters, but how much love we put into it.

REFLECTION — *The objection of Judas*

Mary anointed the feet of Jesus with nard, an expensive, fragrant oil. It was a wonderful gesture on her part. But one of the guests, Judas, took exception to it. He reckoned the nard was worth three hundred denarii – the equivalent of a year's wage for a working man. He said the perfume should have been sold and the money given to the poor.

A noble sentiment, if he meant it. But he didn't. Whereas Mary's expression of appreciation for Jesus was genuine, Judas's expression of concern for the poor wasn't. St John tells us that Judas wasn't thinking of the poor but of himself. He was in charge of their funds, and used to help himself to the contributions they got from the people.

Still, Judas' objection had some objective validity, despite his vile motives. The same objection is often made in good faith by those for whom religion consists only in social action.

As usual Jesus' first concern was for the person in front of him. A love like Mary's demanded expression. So he said to Judas, 'Leave her alone. You have the poor with you always. But I won't be with you always.' This means that there is a place for service to the poor; but there must also be a place for expressing our love for our friends.

But Jesus was also challenging those who claimed to be concerned about the poor. In effect he was saying to them: 'If you are truly concerned about the poor, you can help them any time you choose, because there are always poor among you.'

Saint John tells us that the scent of Mary's perfume filled the entire house. By including the story in his Gospel, he has made it possible for it to fill the entire world.

REFLECTION — *The ability to receive*

Some people are very generous in giving to others. But the same people are not always good at receiving from others.

First of all it has to be said that giving is at the heart of the Gospel. However, there can be a danger in giving. Giving inflates the ego. Therefore, self-love can enter into it. If one is not careful one can end up serving oneself rather than others.

Now while giving is important, so too is receiving. We all need to receive – from others and above all from God. Of ourselves we are incomplete. Even Jesus needed to receive. We see an example of this in today's Gospel.

Martha and Mary had given a dinner in his honour. Martha as usual was waiting at table. But it fell to Mary to make the most extraordinary gesture. She anointed his feet with ointment, doing so with a generosity that bordered on the reckless. She wanted to let him know how much she loved him.

Judas thought she had gone overboard and tried to stop her. But Jesus said, 'Let her be.' He received the kindness and hospitality of the two sisters with great graciousness. Their kindness was a welcome relief from the mounting hostility of the religious leaders.

Here Jesus teaches us how to receive. It is only those who know how to receive who know how to give. It takes a good person to receive a gift well. When we receive with graciousness we do wonders for the giver. We give the giver a chance to love and to enter the world of sharing.

Giving and receiving are both graced activities. But there has to be a balance between them. When we give cheerfully, and receive gratefully, everyone is blessed.

PRAYER OF THE FAITHFUL

Celebrant: In a spirit of trust, let us now bring our needs before the Lord.

Response: Lord, hear us in your love.

Reader(s): That Christians may be known for their generosity and hospitality. [Pause] We pray in faith.

For those who look after the sick and the dying: that they may have gentle hands and warm hearts. [Pause] We pray in faith.

For begrudgers and criticisers: that they may undergo a change of heart. [Pause] We pray in faith.

For grace not be afraid to show our friends how much we love and appreciate them. [Pause] We pray in faith.

For grace to be grateful for the kindnesses done to us by others. [Pause] We pray in faith.

For all gathered here: that the Passion of Jesus may help us to shoulder our burdens and not to lose heart. [Pause] We pray in faith.

For our own special needs. [Longer pause] We pray in faith.

Celebrant: Lord our God, help us to keep our hearts pure, our minds clean, our words true, and our deeds kind. We ask this through Christ our Lord.

REFLECTION

The scent of Mary's perfume filled the entire house.
Yet, in itself, her gesture was a small one.
But small deeds are very important.
They may not look much,
but they create a friendly atmosphere.
They remind us of small flowers.
Small flowers give off little scent on their own,
but put a bunch of them together,
and they can fill a room with fragrance.

TUESDAY OF HOLY WEEK

INTRODUCTION AND CONFITEOR

Jesus was wounded for our sins. We too are wounded by sin – by our own sins and by the sins of others. Let us bring our wounds to the Lord, and ask him for pardon and healing. [Pause]

Lord Jesus, you heal the wounds of sin and division. Lord, have mercy.

You reconcile us to one another and to the Father. Christ, have mercy.

You plead for us at the right hand of the Father. Lord, have mercy.

SCRIPTURE NOTE

Today's *First Reading* (Is 49:1-6) contains the second of the Servant Songs. This is addressed to the Gentile nations. It stresses the early call and formation of the servant. Even though he feels that his mission has been a failure, he doesn't lose his zeal but trusts that God will reveal the fruit of it in his own time. He learns to seek his only reward in God, who is his strength. God assures him that not only will he lead back Jacob and reassemble and teach Israel, but he will be a light for all nations, enabling God's salvation to reach to the ends of the earth.

The *Gospel* (Jn 13:21-33.36-38) tells how the final conflict between God and Satan began. The first move on the part of the powers of evil came from within the circle of friends Jesus had chosen. Even though this caused him to be 'troubled in spirit', he refused to expose Judas. Instead, he gave him a morsel of bread (a gesture of friendship). After receiving this token of friendship, Judas went out into the night. The night symbolises the darkness that had already taken possession of his soul.

Jesus now talks about his glorification. He speaks of it as something that has already happened, because the train of events that led to it has begun. In typical fashion, Peter wants to short-circuit the whole demand of Jesus, and go straight with him to glory. But Jesus, who knows Peter better than he knows himself, forecasts that before the night is out, he will have denied him three times.

REFLECTIONS — *Judas, the betrayer*

The Gospel says that Jesus was 'deeply disturbed' at the thought of being betrayed by one of his own. It's not surprising. He had personally chosen and trained Judas. Judas had heard his teaching and witnessed his miracles. Yet now he was about to betray him. The treachery of a friend is much more hurtful than the treachery of an enemy.

Those who have been betrayed can take comfort from the fact that Jesus knows how they feel. They do not have to pretend that they are not affected by it. Jesus showed how hurt he was, and talked openly about it. What matters is how we deal with the hurt. It could make us bitter and tempt us to retaliate.

In spite of feeling hurt, Jesus did not hit back at Judas. He even refused to expose him in front of the others. Thus he left the door open for him to return to the fold. But in giving him a morsel of bread (a gesture of friendship), he let him know that he knew what he was planning.

Alas, Judas was past the point of rescue. He left the room and went out into the dark night. But darkness was nothing new to him. The moment he decided to betray Jesus, he left the light and passed into darkness.

Like all evil-doers, Judas is an enigmatic figure. We'll never know for sure what motivated him. But it's scary to think that he was exposed to all that Jesus had to offer, yet it came to nothing.

We have to come to terms with the fact that there is a dark side to us too. We must not be frighten of our dark side or depressed about it. But we ignore it at our peril. However, there is also a bright side to us. We must try to live out of this bright side while not forgetting the dark side.

REFLECTIONS — *Peter's brave words*

Jesus said that he was going away. Without knowing where Jesus was going, Peter declared that he was ready to follow him, ready even to lay down his life for him.

Brave words! But Jesus wasn't taken in by them. He knew Peter better than Peter knew himself. He said, 'So you're ready to lay down your life for me! Before the cock crows you will have denied me three times.'

Peter loved Jesus and assumed that his love would endure anything. He was not aware of his own weakness. By next morning he had learned a bitter but salutary lesson.

In talking about the denials of Peter, Jesus didn't show the same hurt as when talking about the betrayal of Judas. But of course there is a world of difference between the two things. Judas' betrayal was a planned thing, and involved real malice. Peter's denial was not a planned thing. It was the result of weakness rather than malice.

What we are and what we think we are, are two very different things. The discovery of what we are can be a soul-shattering experience. But the great thing about Peter was that when he fell, he repented immediately and learned from the experience. Judas, on the other hand, was not able to face what he had done, and decided to end it all.

In learning about Peter, we learn about ourselves too. We may not be as strong, or as courageous, or as generous as we think we are. Peter fell not because he was weak, but because he thought he was strong. He shows us the danger of presumption.

More important still, the incident shows us what Jesus is like. Though he knows our weakness and can foresee our falls, he doesn't write us off. When we fall, he helps us to learn from the experience and to go forward again, relying this time on his strength rather than our own.

REFLECTIONS — *Darkness of heart*

Judas was chosen to be a witness to the light, yet he ended up in darkness. Can we shed any light on his journey into darkness?

We can presume that his heart was bright to begin with, bright with idealism and generosity. He didn't suddenly turn against Jesus. There must have been a gradual dimming of the light. One doesn't suddenly become a scoundrel, unless one has already been one in the making. His journey into the night began some time back. But it was only on the last night that the full extent of the darkness became apparent.

He knew what he was doing. His act was not the result of a sudden impulse or fit of passion. It was a planned thing, and was carried out in a cold, calculating manner. Moreover, he saw how it affected Jesus. Nevertheless, he went ahead with it.

Judas became something worse than an enemy. He became a traitor. But he didn't set out to become a traitor. Nor did God predestine him for that role. He became a traitor through the choices he made. He set out with a dream. But something went wrong. What exactly that was we'll never know. The only clue the Gospel gives us is that before he became a traitor he became a thief (John 12:6).

No one has ever explained what motivated Judas to do what he did. But one thing is clear: Jesus never rejected him. On the contrary, he loved him to the end. Probably the worst thing Judas did was to despair.

Judas must have once been a good man. This is what frightens us. When we look at him we see something of ourselves, of our cowardice, our failures, our betrayals, and our need of grace. All of us have a dark side. There are many degrees of darkness and many shades of night, but darkness of heart is the blackest night of all.

PRAYER OF THE FAITHFUL

Celebrant: The Lord is our light and our help. Let us bring our needs before him with confidence.

Response: Lord, hear our prayer.

Reader(s): For the followers of Christ: that they may have the courage and strength to profess their faith openly. [Pause] Let us pray to the Lord.

For those who have been let down by others, and who are bitter as a result. [Pause] Let us pray to the Lord.

For the conversion of those who are living in the darkness of evil. [Pause] Let us pray to the Lord.

For grace to learn from Peter how to repent of our sins. [Pause] Let us pray to the Lord.

For our own special needs. [Longer pause] Let us pray to the Lord.

Celebrant: God of power and love, fill our hearts with your love. Give us the grace to rise above our human weakness, and keep us faithful to you and to one another. We ask this through Christ our Lord.

REFLECTION

This week we recall the Passion of Jesus.
The fact that Jesus could and did suffer,
means that he understands our suffering,
and gives a meaning to it by showing
that it is the price of love and the path to glory.
In the fragile humanity which he shared with us,
he bore the wounds of love and fidelity.
He gives courage and hope to all who suffer,
but especially to those who suffer in the cause of right.

WEDNESDAY OF HOLY WEEK

INTRODUCTION AND CONFITEOR

God is the help of those who suffer, especially those who suffer in the cause of right. God's unfailing support gives them the strength to persevere, confident that they can triumph over evil. Let us come to the Lord, asking his help in our own struggle with evil. [Pause]

Lord Jesus, you were pierced for our faults. Lord, have mercy.
You bore our sufferings and sorrows. Christ, have mercy.
Through your wounds we are healed. Lord, have mercy.

SCRIPTURE NOTE

Today's *First Reading* (Is 50: 4-9) contains the third of the Servant Songs. The servant must first be a disciple, prayerfully receiving God's word, before presuming to teach others. His message evidently meets with opposition and results in persecution. But he absorbs all the physical and mental abuse directed at him without retaliating. The insults don't really touch him, because he is confident that God will help and vindicate him. (As we read this passage we think of Jesus standing alone and unarmed before Caiphas, Herod, and Pilate).

The *Gospel* (Mt 26:14-25) tells how Judas went to the chief priest, offering to hand Jesus over to them, and was paid thirty silver pieces for doing so. Matthew sees in this the fulfilment of a prophecy in Zechariah (11:12). Thus, even in the treachery of Judas, the things that had been written about the Son of Man are being fulfilled.

Then we read about the preparations for the Passover meal. During it Jesus tells the apostles that one of them will betray him. This causes them great distress, and they want to know who the traitor is. The death of Jesus was inevitable; he is going to his death in accordance with the scriptures and the will of God. But it is not inevitable that one of his disciples should betray him.

The words 'It would be better for that man if he had never been born' are terrible words. But no doubt they were meant as a warning and not as a threat. Jesus discloses to Judas alone that he knows who the traitor is. In refusing to name him in front of the others, he was leaving the door open for him to return to the fold.

REFLECTION — *Moment of truth for Judas*

What Judas did was a horrible, foul deed. Betrayal! Is there a sorrier word in all of sacred scripture? The fact that he knew Jesus was innocent made it worse.

His sin was not the result of a sudden impulse or fit of passion. It was a planned thing, and was carried out in a cold, calculating matter. He knew what he was doing. Moreover, he saw how it affected Jesus, as well as the distress it caused his fellow apostles. Nevertheless, he went ahead with it.

Judas didn't set out to become a traitor. There must have been good in him, otherwise Jesus would not have chosen him in the first place. And it's clear that he wasn't evil through and through, because when he saw that Jesus had been condemned to death, he realised what he had done and regretted it. He threw back the money saying, 'I have sinned in betraying an innocent man.'

Judas didn't suddenly turn against Jesus. His decision to betray him was not a spur-of-the-moment thing. There had been a gradual slipping, a gradual dimming of the light, a gradual loss of faith. On this night he merely came out from the shadows and showed himself in his true colours.

In the final analysis, probably the worst thing he did was to despair of forgiveness. He teaches us a lesson. Dark evil sleeps in us all. The dimming of the light begins with a step which may appear to be of no seeming consequence – just one of those small acts of cowardice with which all the terrible things of the world begin.

REFLECTION — *Loved to the end*

The night before he died Jesus sat at table with his apostles. At a certain point he looked at them and said sadly, 'One of you is about to betray me.' He was deeply upset. He had personally chosen and trained these men. They had heard all his teaching and witnessed all his miracles. Yet one of them was about to betray him.

Now it was the turn of the apostles to get upset. It grieved them to think that one of their number could do such a thing. In betraying Jesus, the betrayer was betraying them too. One after another they asked, 'Is it I, Master?' This shows that they realised (as we should) that each carried the potential for treachery.

Taking a piece of bread, Jesus said, 'It is the man to whom I will give this piece of bread. Alas for the man by whom the Son of Man is betrayed. It would be better for him if he had never been born.' These are terrible words. No doubt they were meant as a warning and not as a threat.

Jesus knew what Judas was up to. Yet he refused to expose him in front of the others. Everything remained between him and Judas. Thus he left the door open for him to return to the fold.

A number of times during that last night he tried to reach him. He tried again in the garden. When Judas kissed him he said, 'Judas, my friend, do you betray the Son of Man with a kiss?' Sadly, the words made no impression on Judas. By now he was past the point of rescue.

No one has ever explained what motivated Judas to do what he did. But one thing is clear: Jesus never rejected him. On the contrary, he loved him to the end. But by this is sentence passed on him, that even though he was exposed to the light, he opted for the darkness. Nevertheless, probably the worst thing he did was to despair.

REFLECTION — *The ones who remained faithful*

The betrayal of Judas dominates today's Gospel as it did yesterday's. But we must not forget the other apostles. In spite of stumbling, eleven of them remained faithful to Jesus. That's not a bad percentage. It would not be right, then, to give all the attention to Judas.

It was a terrible night for those eleven apostles – a night of sadness, confusion, and terror. When at the last supper Jesus said that one of them would betray him, they were greatly distressed. It grieved them to think that one of their number could do such a thing.

What Judas did hurt them too. After all, he was one of themselves. He was their fellow disciple, their friend, their brother. They had trusted him, and shared everything with him. They thought they knew him, and yet he turned out to be a traitor. In betraying Jesus he betrayed them too.

But as yet they did not know who the traitor was. So each of them in turn asked, 'Is it I, Lord?' This shows that they realised (as we should) that each carried the potential for treachery. No one is so strong that he can't fall.

Evil depresses us. Good, on the other hand, inspires us. On that night of trial, the behaviour of the apostles shows us the two sides of human nature – the capacity for betrayal, and the capacity for fidelity.

These two sides, these two potentialities, are within each of us. Each of us can be weak, cowardly, and selfish. But then each of us is capable of being strong, brave, and generous. We are a mixture of light and darkness. We have to work hard to ensure that the light triumphs over the darkness. But in the end, only the grace of God can guarantee this.

PRAYER OF THE FAITHFUL

Celebrant: With confidence in God's goodness, let us now brings our needs before him.

Response: Lord, graciously hear us

Reader(s): For Christians: that they may not be deterred by their own weakness. [Pause] Lord, hear us.

For sinners: that they may have the courage to acknowledge their sins, and the grace to rise from them. [Pause] Lord, hear us.

For all gathered here: that the knowledge of our own failures may make us understanding towards those who fall. [Pause] Lord, hear us.

For grace to draw inspiration from the good example of others. [Pause] Lord, hear us.

For our own special needs. [Longer pause] Lord, hear us.

Celebrant: Lord Jesus, be our companion on the road of life. Do not go ahead of, we may not follow; do not walk behind us, we may not lead; just walk beside us and be our friend. We make this prayer to the Father through you Christ our Lord.

REFLECTION

When we are mistreated retaliation is not the answer;
retaliation only adds darkness to darkness.
Jesus shows us a better way.
When he was mistreated he did not retaliate.
He didn't lash out at Judas.
Instead, he loved him to the end.
Jesus challenges us to respond to darkness with light.
The way he proposes is not a soft way.
It is a hard way, but it is a better way.

Appendix

HOLY THURSDAY:

MASS OF THE LORD'S SUPPER

INTRODUCTION AND CONFITEOR

On the night before he died, Jesus gathered his apostles around him and ate the Passover meal with them. That meal is the origin of the Eucharist. On this special evening, we gather around the table of the Lord. Let us reflect for a moment on how we live out our unity with Christ and one another. [Pause]

Lord Jesus, lamb without blemish, sacrificed for us: Lord, have mercy.

Goodness beyond our power to repay: Christ, have mercy.

Master and teacher of love and of service: Lord, have mercy.

SCRIPTURE NOTE

The *First Reading* (Ex 12:1–8.11–14) tells us about the origin of the Passover meal, which marked the deliverance of the Israelites from Egypt. At each Passover, Israel looked backward to the first Passover and forward to the final deliverance which God had promised. The Passover was a memorial recalling God's fidelity to his covenant, and an assurance that God would be faithful to his promises.

The *Second Reading* (1 Cor 11:23-26) contains the earliest written account of the origin of the Eucharist. In the Eucharist we re-enact the death by which Jesus saved us. It is not just a repetition: it is a re-presentation. It takes yesterday's action and makes it live again in all its aspects. The Eucharist is the memorial of the death and resurrection of Jesus. At each Eucharist we look back to his death and forward to his coming again.

The *Gospel* (Jn 13:1-15) is a scene from the Last Supper. Jesus is about to give the apostles the supreme manifestation of his love – laying down his life for them. But first he performs an act of humble service – he washes their feet. As their acknowledged Lord and Master, he has authority over them. But his style and exercise of authority is marked by service. Humble service must also characterise the lives of his disciples.

REFLECTION — *A symbolic act*

Sometimes words are not enough to convey an important truth. In that case we resort to gestures which can convey the truth more forcefully: actions speak louder than words.

To take an example we are all familiar with. Before Communion we are asked to offer one another a sign of peace. We say to one another: 'Peace be with you.' But we also give one another a handshake. That handshake is a symbolic gesture. I think it gets the message across more forcefully than any words we might say.

A symbolic gesture shouldn't need to be explained; it should speak for itself. But sometimes due to cultural factors a word of explanation may be needed.

This brings us to this evening, and to the gesture Jesus made when he washed the feet of the apostles. The roads of Palestine were just dirt roads. After a journey the travellers' feet (or sandals) were covered in dust. A servant was standing by to wash and dry the feet of the guests as they arrived. Cool water was poured over the feet to cleanse and soothe them. This menial but important task fell to the lowest servant.

On that night Jesus took on the role of that servant and washed the feet of the apostles. The meaning would have been clear to them. It was so radical that Peter objected to it. He didn't think it was right that Jesus should assume that role and perform that lowly task. But Jesus insisted on going ahead with it.

Then to make sure they grasped the meaning of what he had done he said to them: 'You call me Master and Lord, and rightly; so I am. If I, then, the Lord and Master, have washed your feet, you should wash each other's feet. I have given you an example so that you may copy what I have done to you.'

But a gesture could be a powerful one and still be an empty one, if there is no commitment present. In Jesus' case it wasn't just a gesture. This was how he had always acted towards them. 'The Son of Man came not to be served but to serve … and to give his life as a ransom for many' (Mt 20:28).

His chief concern that night was to show the kind of leadership he wanted in his community. He wanted the leaders to be the servants of their brothers and sisters. Alas, this great lesson got lost down the centuries. Christians leaders expected others to serve them. Thankfully, we are recovering it in our times.

Humble service is something that should characterise the lives of all disciples. However, service of itself won't ennoble us unless we can do it with love. It has to be an expression of love. Forced service leads only to bitterness and resentment.

True communion among Christians is possible only in an atmosphere of loving service. The Eucharist is at the centre of everything. It is this that binds them together and enables them to offer loving service to one another.

REFLECTION — *The Eucharist and Service*

At the Last Supper Jesus told the disciples to share the Eucharist in memory of him, and to serve one another. This shows that there is an intimate connection between the Eucharist and service.

We must never forget that the Jesus we receive in the Eucharist is the same Jesus who gave his life for us. The words of the consecration remind us of this: 'This is my body given for you … This is my blood shed for you.' To receive this food is to be reminded that, like Jesus, we too must be willing to give ourselves in the service of others.

Someone who understood this very well was Mother Teresa. She said: 'We see the love and care with which the priest touches Jesus in the Host during Mass. We must show the same love and respect for the broken bodies of the poor, because it is the same Jesus we find there. When we wash and clean their wounds we are touching the body of Christ.'

Jesus chose to wash the feet of his disciples. He did what a servant would do. We who bear his name must live lives of loving service. Unless we surround the breaking of the bread and the sharing of the cup with acts of loving service, we will be left with a static ritual that will no longer inspire and nourish us.

The Eucharist is the heart of everything. But it can never be separated from the washing of the feet. The two realities are linked. Being in communion with Jesus must mean being in communion with others. Jesus gives himself to us here, so that we in our turn may give ourselves to others.

The first Christians understood this very well. Hence, they supported one another. They forgave each other's offences, shared their possessions, and fostered the spirit of community. The Eucharist was at the centre of everything. It was this that bound them together and enabled them to offer loving service to one another. Sharing creates a bond, and bonding leads to sharing.

REFLECTION — *The commandment of love*

During the Last Supper, knowing that he was soon to leave them, Jesus left the apostles a new commandment to live by: 'Love one another as I have loved you.' It is new only in the sense that it sets a new standard – 'as I have loved you'. The world will know that they are his disciples by their fidelity to this commandment.

Of all the commandments Jesus gave us this is the most important. It includes all the others. The only failure in the life of a Christian is the failure to love. It is not an easy commandment. We know how difficult it is to take some people into our hearts. But Jesus himself set the example for us to follow.

Earlier that night he had said to them, 'Tonight all of you will abandon me' (Mt 26:31). And, deeply distressed, he had said, 'One of you is about to betray me' (Mt 26:21). Was it not a strange time, then, to talk about love when love was being betrayed? It is precisely at a time like this that love has to prove itself.

Jesus foresaw that the apostles would abandon him later that night. He foresaw that Peter would deny him and that Judas would betray him. Betrayal is a terribly thing. Few if any relationships can survive it. Yet Jesus refused to shut them out of his heart. Instead, he went on loving them. We have to realise that it was a difficult night for the apostles too, a night of sadness, confusion, and fear.

In calling us to love, Jesus is not laying a burden on us. Rather, he is calling us to life. He is calling us to open our hearts, and to open the heart is to begin to live.

Love always demands the best of us, and brings out the best in us. 'Love is the flame that warms our soul, energises our spirit, and supplies passion to our lives' (Elizabeth Kubler-Ross).

Those who do not love have an impoverished life. But those who do love have a fruitful life. Love is well-being. Love makes us fruitful. To refuse to love is to begin to die. To begin to love is to begin to live.

There is an intimate connection between the Eucharist and the commandment to love. Mother Teresa said: 'The Jesus we find in the consecrated host is the same Jesus we find in the broken bodies of our poor.'

To be able to make this kind of connection we need the help of the Lord himself. It is above all in the Eucharist that he gives us this help. Mother Teresa put it like this: 'In the Eucharist I receive the spiritual food which sustains me in all my labours. Without it I could not get through one single day or hour of my life.'

PRAYER OF THE FAITHFUL

Celebrant: Gathered around the table of the Lord on this special evening, let us bring before him our own needs, the needs of the Church, and of the world.

Response: Lord, graciously hear us.

Reader(s): For the Church: that the Eucharist may form its members into a community of love. [Pause] Lord, hear us.

For the world: that all of God's family may be gathered together in unity and peace. [Pause] Lord, hear us.

For all those who minister in the Church: that they may be filled with Christlike love. [Pause] Lord, hear us.

For those who have cut themselves off from the Church: that they may be drawn back into communion with it. [Pause] Lord, hear us.

For the sick, the lonely, and the unloved: that in their pain they may know God's comforting. [Pause] Lord, hear us.

For our departed relatives and friends, who partook of the Eucharist: that they may enjoy the banquet of eternal life in heaven. [Pause] Lord, hear us.

For our own special needs. [Longer pause] Lord, hear us.

Celebrant: God of love and mercy, you sent Jesus your Son to be the servant of all. Grant that the food we eat at the table of the Eucharist may make us strong, so that we may follow his example by offering loving service to one another. Grant this through Christ our Lord.

SIGN OF PEACE

Lord Jesus Christ, the night before you died you said to your apostles: 'Peace I leave with you, my own peace I give you. A peace which the world cannot give, this is my gift to you. So do not let your hearts be troubled or afraid.' Take pity on our troubled and fearful hearts, and grant us the peace and unity of your kingdom where you live for ever and ever.

PRAYER AFTER COMMUNION

Heavenly Father, the bread we have eaten in the Eucharist was once scattered over the fields in the form of grains of wheat, but then was gathered together and became one loaf. So may your Church be gathered together from the ends of the earth into your Kingdom.

To you belong glory and power through Jesus Christ, for ever and ever. Amen.

Saints' Days

Vincent Ryan

Readings for Saints' Days

The *General Introduction to the Lectionary for Mass* (1981) makes it clear that readings assigned in the weekday lectionary 'are to be read on the days to which they are assigned except on the days when there is a solemnity, a feast or a memorial with its own proper readings.' (n. 82)

For most memorials, the readings shown in the lectionary are indicative only, and do not necessarily displace the *lectio continua* provided in the weekday lectionary. When the following pages offer commentary on readings for optional memorials or for memorials, this does not amount to advice that those readings should be used. Rather, such commentary is designed to help elucidate aspects of the life and witness of the saint.

February

REFLECTION

One of the most beautiful sections in the *Life of St Benedict*, attributed to Pope St Gregory the Great, is that which describes the saintly abbot's relationship with his sister Scholastica, herself a consecrated virgin. It is an account of their last meeting, about 547 AD, at a spot close to Monte Cassino. They spent the whole day singing God's praises and conversing about the spiritual life. When Benedict judged it time to be going back to his monastery, Scholastica entreated him to stay. When he would not she had recourse to a holy ruse. She prayed for and obtained a rain-storm. St Benedict, unable to stir out of the house, accepted his predicament in good part. The result was that brother and sister spent the whole night 'in holy converse about the interior life'.

The story, which can be read in the Breviary, is a kind of parable. In a spiritual contest between two holy people, the power of love prevailed. On the one hand, there is St Benedict, the monastic legislator, concerned about a possible infringement of the Rule. On the other, hand we have Scholastica, less constrained by rules and regulations, readier to follow the promptings of her heart. The result of the contest is summed up in a lapidary phrase: 'she was able to obtain more who loved more' – '*Plus valuit quae amplius amavit*'. Is there a gentle chiding here of over-punctilious people? In any case, the Gospel is the Rule of Rules, and love is the supreme law.

What is so attractive about St Scholastica is the purity of her love. It manifested itself at an early age. She had been 'consecrated to God from early childhood'. It was so pure and strong that it could even obtain miracles. The prayer of the day speaks of 'unsullied love' (*intemerata caritas*). This is confirmed by the saint's life and by her holy death. A few days after the eventful meeting described above, St Benedict saw the soul of his sister ascending to heaven in the form of a dove.

Today's feast celebrates a friendship, one that is deeply spiritual and profoundly human. The call to religious life does not mean that family ties are irreversibly severed. There may be an initial distancing from parents, brothers and sisters; but having made the sacrifice of those we hold dearest, we find them again in a new and more perfect form. That is part of the promised 'hundredfold'. When brother and sister follow a similar call and aspire to the same ideal, their mutual friendship can be a powerful support in their pilgrimage of faith. Scholastica and Benedict remained united in death: 'Their bodies share a common resting place, just as in life their souls had always been one in God'.

PETITION FOR THE PRAYER OF THE FAITHFUL

That we may learn from St Scholastica how to love God with undivided hearts, while cherishing and fostering family ties and human friendships.

11 February
OUR LADY OF LOURDES

Optional Memorial

REFLECTION

Lourdes is one of the greatest centres of pilgrimage in modern times, and undoubtedly the most popular of Marian shrines. It was on this day in the year 1858 that Our Lady first appeared to the fourteen-year-old girl, Bernadette Soubirous. At first the child did not know who the mysterious lady was. Later she was to learn that it was the Blessed Virgin, and to hear from her lips: 'I am the Immaculate', on December 8.

Lourdes has become a place of healing – not necessarily physical, although there are authenticated miracles. Lourdes itself is a kind of miracle, manifested in the faith and devotion of the people who go there and in the selfless spirit of service of the volunteers who work there. In a world where people do not want to know about their suffering brothers and sisters, and would keep the sick and infirm out of sight, here at Lourdes these afflicted ones are honoured citizens and the object of love and attention. In 1992 Pope John Paul II instituted the World Day of the Sick, to be held each year on the memorial of Our Lady of Lourdes.

An alternative *First Reading* (Is 66) is provided for Mass. It presents Jerusalem as a loving mother tenderly nurturing her children – a symbol of the Church and of Mary, mother of Christ and of his Church. This maternal role of the Church and of Mary is seen at its best in places like Lourdes where people are united in prayer and in service of one another; where there is a great deal of caring, and where the sacraments of Penance, Eucharist and Anointing of the Sick are celebrated with such faith and devotion.

'Now towards her I send flowing peace like a river'. Those who do not receive physical healing at Lourdes, are sure to find that inner peace and refreshment of which the prophet speaks. They find strength and serenity in their illness, and hope to face the future. Lourdes is a place of reconciliation and of spiritual healing. Through a poor peasant girl Mary called sinners to repentance. And we ask today that God may 'grant us through her prayer strength in our weakness and grace to rise from our sins'.

PETITION FOR THE PRAYER OF THE FAITHFUL

For all pilgrims to Lourdes, especially the infirm in mind or body. Through the intercession of Mary, 'Mother of the sick', may they receive the healing they long for.

14 February

SAINT CYRIL, Monk, and SAINT METHODIUS, Bishop

Feast in Europe

REFLECTION

These two Greek-born brothers lived in the ninth century. Becoming priests at Constantinople, they set out in 863 as missionaries to the Slav people in Moravia, a region that corresponds to the present-day Czech and Slovak republics. In this mission they were enterprising and innovative, preaching and celebrating the liturgy in Slavonic and devising a new alphabet for that language. Unfortunately, they met with much mistrust and opposition from their fellow-clergy who did not share their vision. Cyril ended his short life as a professed monk, while his brother became Archbishop of Pannonia, a region corresponding to modern Hungary. There, he continued the evangelization of the Slavs in spite of obstruction and even imprisonment.

The achievements of the saints are not to be measured by the yardstick of worldly success. Humanly speaking, Cyril and Methodius may seem to have failed in their mission. But in God's sight they achieved the task entrusted to them. The seed must fall into the ground and die before the slender shoot and then the ear of corn appears. The harvest would come later. These brothers are rightly acclaimed as the Apostles of the Slavs. The prayer of the feast acknowledges that they 'brought the light of the Gospel to the Slavonic peoples'. No wonder that Pope John Paul II, himself a Slav, should declare these saints Patrons of Europe along with St Benedict. (In Europe their Mass is celebrated as a *festum*.)

It is as apostles of unity, bridging the gap between East and West that their chief importance lies. Their feast-day is celebrated both by the Roman Church and by the Slav Churches of the Byzantine rite. Today our thoughts turn to the Christians of Central and Eastern Europe, as well as to the Orthodox Church in Russia. Since the beginning of the Great Schism nearly a thousand years ago, Eastern and Western Christendom have been divided. In our time the process of healing and reconciliation advances slowly and painfully but with growing understanding and mutual respect.

At the Office of Readings we have a section from the Slavonic *Life of St Cyril*. It contains his dying prayer: 'Make your Church grow in number, and gather all its members into unity. Make them a chosen people, of one mind in your true faith and in orthodox profession'. These words and sentiments are woven into the prayer of the day. We say it in the hope that God in his own time will bring about the re-unification of our Churches.

PETITION FOR THE PRAYER OF THE FAITHFUL

For the Christians of Eastern Europe and Russia who suffer for their faith. May Saints Cyril and Methodius, who laboured for their conversion, obtain for them the courage and steadfastness which they themselves showed.

17 February
THE SEVEN FOUNDERS OF THE SERVITE ORDER
OF THE BLESSED VIRGIN MARY., Religious

Memorial

REFLECTION

In the thirteenth century seven Florentines laid the foundations of what was to become the Order of the Servants of Mary, more generally known as the Servites. A particular object of this Order is to spread devotion to Mary, Mother of the Lord, with special regard to the sorrows she endured during the passion of her Son.

This new religious family encountered many difficulties in its early stages, and indeed it came near to being suppressed. Only one of the founders lived to see the foundation raised to the dignity of a religious order, and that was Alexis, a lay-brother, who died on this day in 1310. The Servite Order had a secure foundation: it was 'built in the beginning by our Lady, founded on the humility of our brothers, with the union of their mind and heart as its fabric, and with poverty as its safeguard' (from the Office of Readings).

The focus of attention is not on the personal lives of these remarkable men who were drawn from the well-to-do merchant class. It is rather on Mary, Mother of Jesus, whose servants they wished to be. They seem to efface themselves in order that she might be better known and loved.

At a time when Marian piety is in decline, or has assumed exaggerated forms, these seven holy founders have an important message for us. From them we can learn the secret of a genuine and balanced devotion to Mary. It is appropriate that we should ask in today's prayer: 'Inspire us, Lord, with the great love the Seven Founders had for Mary, the Mother of God, and as they drew your people to you by their devotion, so may we proclaim your love to all'.

This prayer strikes the right note about devotion to Mary. It is not an end in itself, but is subordinate to devotion to Christ and should lead to a loving service of people. In his encyclical *Marialis Cultus* Pope Paul VI declared that this devotion 'takes its origin and effectiveness from Christ, finds its complete expression in Christ, and leads through Christ in the Spirit to the Father'. It is in this sense that we are true servants of Mary.

PETITION FOR THE PRAYER OF THE FAITHFUL

We pray that the love which the Seven Holy Founders bore Our Lady may also be ours. May it be a force for renewal in our own lives and in the life of the Church.

21 February
SAINT PETER DAMIAN, Bishop and Doctor of the Church

Memorial

REFLECTION

Here is a saint who represents the austere face of the Church. A man who made extreme demands on himself and was exigent of others. The fact that he was orphaned at an early age and suffered ill treatment by one of his brothers no doubt played a part in his psychological development.

Born at Ravenna in 1007, he received a good education and seemed destined for a brilliant academic career. Instead of that he joined the very austere community of Camaldolese monks at Fonte Avellana when he was twenty-eight years of age. In the company of these hermit monks he devoted himself to prayer, penance, theological study and writing. After some years he was elected abbot. His outstanding qualities of leadership were not long in being recognized. In 1057 he was made cardinal-bishop of Ostia, and in that capacity worked strenuously by his writing and preaching to reform abuses in the Church. But he always hankered after the life of prayer and solitude, and was eventually allowed to return to his monastery where he died in 1072.

We may not be greatly drawn by the austere and uncompromising character of Peter Damian. He seems to lack the winning human personality of other saints. One suspects that he was not an easy person to live with! And yet there was another side to his character. We are told that he was kind to his monks and merciful to penitents. The Office of Readings includes a letter written by him to a friend in distress. It could not have failed to bring consolation. He urges his friend to 'wait gladly for the joy that follows sadness'.

A great monk and man of the Church! His reforming zeal was much needed at a time of great laxity in ecclesiastical and monastic life. Like other great monk-bishops he had to reconcile the monastic vocation with the demands of the apostolic ministry. The tension arising from the apparent conflict of these different vocations was resolved by the saint's obedience to the will of God as manifested to him by the Vicar of Christ. In his resolve to do only God's will he found inner peace and equilibrium. And through his obedience he became a great power for good in the medieval Church.

The prayer of the day delicately alludes to this twofold vocation: 'Teach us by the example and doctrine of St Peter Damian to prefer nothing whatever to Christ, and to make the service of the Church our chief concern'. The phrase 'to prefer nothing whatever to Christ' is taken from chapter 32 of the Rule of St Benedict, and represents the great ideal of the monastic vocation. Then 'to make the service of the Church our chief concern' represents the apostolic ideal. We cannot all be monks, reformers, great ascetics – but love of Christ and of his Church, and the readiness to be of service to both, these are incumbent on every Christian.

PETITION FOR THE PRAYER OF THE FAITHFUL

By the example of St Peter Damian may we learn the narrow way that leads to life, and gain the courage to take up our cross and to follow Christ.

22 February
THE CHAIR OF ST PETER, Apostle

Feast

REFLECTION

The historical origins of this feast are rather obscure. The date coincides with an ancient pagan commemoration. On this day the Romans celebrated the *cara cognitio*, the commemoration day of all their beloved dead ones. They gathered round the family tombs and shared a ritual meal with the departed who were represented by an empty chair. Around the middle of the fourth century the Church instituted the feast-day of St Peter's Chair, *Natale Petri de Cathedra*. Thus an ancient commemoration of the dead was transformed into a festival of the Prince of Apostles. The Christians of Rome venerated on this day the memory of their first bishop. His presence too was symbolized by his chair or *cathedra*.

A cathedral is the church where the bishop of a diocese has his seat. It is from here that he presides over the liturgy of the diocesan Church. The chair or throne symbolizes the episcopal office. The occupant may change but the function remains. According to our Catholic faith, the successor of St Peter is the Bishop of Rome. We acknowledge him to be the visible representative of Christ on earth, possessing full and universal jurisdiction in the Church. The unity of the Church is founded on St Peter, according to St Cyprian. The papacy is a guarantee of security, permanence and unity in the Church.

For Pope St Leo, whose words we hear in the Office of Readings, St Peter is no mere figure of the past, but a living presence in the Church. He continues to feed his sheep, to strengthen his flock and to intercede for it in prayer. And this he does collectively with the other Apostles. He and the rest of the Twelve continue to have an active role in the Church: 'From their place in heaven they guide us still' (Preface of Apostles).

The liturgy lays great stress on the faith of St Peter. The Entrance Antiphon cites our Lord's words to Peter: 'I have prayed that your faith may not fail'. The Opening Prayer declares that God has built his Church 'on the rock of St Peter's confession of faith'. This faith is highlighted in both readings and in the Communion Antiphon. In the Prayer over the Gifts we ask: 'With St Peter as our shepherd, keep us true to the faith he taught and bring us to your eternal Kingdom'.

We would do well today to pray for the Pope, successor of the Apostle. I mean really pray, not just acquiesce to his formal mention in the eucharistic prayer and elsewhere. Like St Peter, his faith must be strong enough to 'confirm his brethren'. Yet he does so conscious of his own fragility. It is a daunting task for one man to be responsible for the faith of millions. When Peter was in prison the 'whole Church made intercession for him'. In a sense his successor is also in chains, bound down with the chains of office. Let us pray that neither his faith nor courage may fail. May God be his protection: *Dominus conservet eum.*

PETITIONS FOR THE PRAYER OF THE FAITHFUL

For the Church of Rome: that it may truly 'preside in love', and be seen as a sign of peace and unity in the world.

For our Holy Father, the Pope: that he may be strengthened to bear witness to Christ and his Gospel, and so confirm his brothers and sisters in the faith.

For all Christian leaders: that they may stand firm on the side of truth and justice and be courageous defenders of the poor and oppressed.

23 February

SAINT POLYCARP, Bishop and Martyr

Memorial

REFLECTION

With St Polycarp we bridge the narrow gap separating the age of the Apostles from that of the earliest Church Fathers. For, according to tradition, St Polycarp was a disciple of the Apostle John. He was born about 69 AD and was martyred around 155 AD. He became bishop of Smyrna (a coastal town in what is now Turkey). As a Christian leader he was deeply concerned about orthodoxy of faith and was a vigorous opponent of Gnosticism and other heresies. In old age he was arrested and ordered to renounce his allegiance to Christ. This he refused to do and bravely accepted the consequences: he was condemned to death, slain by the sword and his body burnt. He was revered as a saint in his own lifetime, and the anniversary of his martyrdom was celebrated from the beginning.

In the Office of Readings we have an eye-witness account of the martyrdom of Polycarp. It is a passionate affirmation of his loyalty to Christ: 'Eighty-six years have I served him and he had done me now wrong. How can I blaspheme my King and Saviour?' The whole section needs to be read slowly and reflectively. It breathes the confident assurance and earnest enthusiasm of the early Church. The prayer spoken by Polycarp before his martyrdom is woven of praise, thanksgiving and self-oblation. Some scholars have detected in it the echo of a second-century eucharistic prayer. Indeed the whole narrative has a liturgical character. It amounts to a celebration of martyrdom.

The final oration of the martyr-bishop has inspired other texts in the proper of the feast, in particular the prayer of the day and the *Magnificat* antiphon. Note the allusion to the 'cup of Christ'. We ask: 'May his prayers give us the courage to share with him the cup of suffering and to rise to eternal glory'. We think of our Lord's words to his disciples: 'Have you the strength to drink the cup that I am to drink?' When we receive Communion from the chalice at Mass we might ponder these words. Are we ready to take our share of the sufferings of Christ for the sake of his Church? Are we conscious of the new and eternal Covenant ratified in his blood? It was from the Eucharist that martyrs like Polycarp derived the strength to bear their supreme witness to Christ.

The *Alternative First Reading* (Rev) is a passage in which Jesus addresses the Church at Smyrna. It is a message of encouragement to a community that had endured great trials. The message was still relevant when Polycarp was bishop of that town. It is a solemn assurance that Christ will be with his people in all their trials: 'Even if you have to die, keep faithful, and I will give you the crown of life for your prize'.

PETITION FOR THE PRAYER OF THE FAITHFUL

That our sharing in the Eucharist may fill us with the love

and fortitude that enabled St Polycarp so promptly and joyfully to lay down his life for Christ.

March

1 March
SAINT DAVID, Monk and Bishop

Wales: Feast

REFLECTION

Today Wales celebrates its patron saint. Pilgrims will throng to the town in Pembrokeshire which bears his name, and to its noble cathedral. Here the memory of this great sixth-century monk and bishop is venerated, although his tomb now lies empty. It was at St David's, formerly known as Menevia, that he founded his principal monastery. It is situated at no great distance from Cardigan, traditional birth-place of the saint. After his death there was a rapid extension of his cult. The name of St David is listed for March 1 in the earliest Irish martyrologies.

We know all-too-little about the life of this saint, and some of the later legends have to be discounted. But what we do know about his life and character corresponds to the ascetic ideal so revered by Celtic Christianity. He believed in 'silence, intense manual work and strict mortification'. He was a man of heroic sanctity. But he also practised works of mercy. And as with other Celtic saints cast in this stern mould, there was a gentler and more joyful side. His reputed last words were: 'Be joyful and keep the faith. Do these little things you have seen and heard in me'.

After so many centuries St David remains an inspiring figure for the Church in Wales. The Welsh are a strongly religious people. Religion is very much part of their culture, as is indeed their language which they have tenaciously preserved. Many Christian denominations, mostly of the Non-Conformist kind, are represented. But whatever their allegiance, all Welsh Christians are united in their esteem and love for St David.

Because of the vicissitudes of history, Catholicism had all but become extinct in Wales by the first half of the nineteenth century. The situation might have been quite different if there had been more priests to preach and administer the sacraments. Then, especially in the wake of the Great Famine, there came the great influx of Irish immigrants. The Catholic population grew rapidly, with the result that Wales became a separate Ecclesiastical Province with the Archdiocese of Cardiff as metropolitan and Menevia as its suffragan.

In a time of religious intolerance, ninety-one Welsh Catholics gave their lives for the faith. Today the Church has to contend with subtler and more insidious threats – secularism, a materialist outlook and indifferentism. The Church must pray more than ever before for perseverance in keeping the faith. May Almighty God, through the intercession of St David, 'protect us so that, while we celebrate his festival, we may also imitate his firmness in defending the Catholic faith'.

PETITION FOR THE PRAYER OF THE FAITHFUL
That the Churches in Wales may grow together in unity and in their collective witness to Christ.

4 March
ST CASIMIR, Confessor

Memorial

REFLECTION
St Casimir was born in 1458 at Krakow, son of Casimir IV, King of Poland and Grand-Duke of Lithuania. Throughout his short life – he died of consumption at the age of twenty-six – he dedicated himself wholly to the service of God and of people. His love for the poor was immense. According to a contempo-

rary he was 'a father, son and brother' to widows orphans and the oppressed.

By his fellow-Poles Casimir was called not only 'Defender of the Poor' but also 'Peace-maker'. He had the moral courage to stand up to his father who had military ambitions and wished his son to lead armies into battle. On principle, Casimir would not make war on other Christian nations and was prepared to accept imprisonment as a consequence of his stand. He was a pacifist in the noble sense – not afraid to fight but unwilling to take the lives of others except in self-defence or in a just war.

His remarkable life was sustained by deep prayer, strong devotion to the Blessed Sacrament and to Our Lady. His discipline of life was austere, but in his relations with others he was serene and cheerful, gentle and considerate. He used his authority not to exploit but to serve. The prayer of the feast focuses on this aspect of his life: 'Almighty God, to serve you is to reign with you. At the intercession of St Casimir, grant that we may always serve you by just and holy living'.

St Casimir is principal patron of Lithuania. His tomb is venerated at Vilnius where he died on this day in 1484. Lithuania has been a Christian nation for six hundred years, since the year 1387 when the Grand-Duke Jagellong, having been baptised himself, organised the baptism of his people and founded the diocese of Vilnius.

Lithuania has a population roughly that of the Irish Republic – about three and a half million – of which the great majority are Catholics of the Roman rite. It is a country that has suffered much. For three centuries it was united to Poland, then in 1795 it passed into the Russian empire. From 1918 until the outbreak of the Second World War it enjoyed a brief spell of independence; then it was occupied by the Nazi armies for three years and then annexed by the victorious Russians. After the war it was subjected to violent and systematic persecution. Notwithstanding so much adversity, the Church in that small state has survived. Lithuania is still eighty per cent Catholic. Since 1989, it has become possible to re-establish Catholic structures, with the return of bishops banished by the Soviets and the consecration of new bishops. As it faces new challenges in an era of freedom and Lithuanian membership of the European Union, the Lithuanian Church continues to need our prayers.

PETITION FOR THE PRAYER OF THE FAITHFUL

For the Churches of Poland and Lithuania. May their leaders and people remain steadfast in their allegiance to the Catholic faith, aided by the prayer and example of St Casimir.

7 March
SAINTS PERPETUA AND FELICITY, Martyrs

Memorial

REFLECTION

In an age of martyrs these two women are outstanding for their heroism. Perpetua was a wealthy married woman, while Felicity, her companion, was a slave-girl. Both were undergoing instruction for Baptism in their native Carthage in North Africa. About the year 203 they were arrested with some companions, cruelly tortured and finally executed. An eyewitness account of their martyrdom has come down to us, and it bears witness to their steadfastness and serenity even in the face of torment and death.

What gives a note of poignancy to their story is the fact that Felicity was pregnant at the time of her arrest and gave birth to a girl while in prison. Also one cannot fail to be touched by the tender affection these women bore one another. Their mutual friendship broke down the barriers of social class. They were wholly united in their love for each other and in their love for Christ.

The prayer of the feast extols their victory over the pain of death. And the secret of that victory was their 'overwhelming love'. In one of the responsories of the Office we hear the words of Paul: 'What can separate us from the love of Christ? Can affliction or hardship? Can persecution, hunger, nakedness, peril on the sword' (Rom 8:38-39). The *Magnificat* antiphon for second Vespers continues this theme: 'The saints, who followed in the footsteps of Christ, rejoice in heaven. They gave their life for love of Christ; therefore they will reign with him for ever'.

The martyrs met hatred and violence with love. They were inspired by the example of Christ who, on the cross, won 'the victory of suffering love'. If they were not motivated by love their sacrifice would be in vain; for 'if I even let them take my body to burn it, but am without love, it will do me no good whatever' (1 Cor 13:3). Fanaticism is but a caricature of martyrdom. The martyrs point to the way of non-violence, the way marked out by Christ.

'Do not be overcome by evil, but overcome evil with good' (Rom 12:21). At least there have always been some who have heeded St Paul's injunction and have resisted the temptation to meet force with force, hatred and hatred. For them love has been 'as strong as death', even stronger. Saints Perpetua and Felicity have exemplified such love.

PETITION FOR THE PRAYER OF THE FAITHFUL

For all those who seek peace and justice by non-violence: that they may not be discouraged by failure and misunderstanding, but continue to bear witness to the Gospel of love.

8 March
SAINT JOHN OF GOD, Religious

Memorial

REFLECTION

Born in Portugal in 1495. Choosing a military career, he abandoned all practice of religion. Then at the age of forty he underwent a conversion, and pledged to devote his life to God. There followed a period of groping and emotional turmoil as he strove to know how he might best serve his fellow-men. It was the famous preacher, John of Avila, who pointed the way to his true vocation in life – the care of the sick poor. He opened a hospital in Granada where, until his death in 1580, he devoted himself to the care of the physically and mentally ill, especially the very poor. After his death his followers were formed into a religious order, that of the Hospitallers of St John of God.

'Compassion' is the word that best characterises John of God's life and ministry. It springs to mind as we read his own words in the Office of Readings: 'When I see so many of my brethren in poverty, and my neighbours suffering beyond their strength, and oppressed in mind and body by so many cares, and am unable to help them, it causes me exceeding sorrow'. Compassion is the note sounded in the Prayer: 'Lord, you filled the heart of St John of God with compassion for his fellow-men'.

'Be compassionate just as you Father is compassionate' (Lk 6:36). John of God responded totally to that command. It is one which constantly challenges us, and is echoed in the exhortation of St Paul: 'Be clothed in heartfelt compassion' (Col 3:12). A Gospel value of vital importance, it must at all times be evident in the lives of Christians. Among the Fathers of the Church, St John Chrysostom preached on it with particular insistence and eloquence. In one of his homilies he places these words on the lips of Christ: 'Be touched by compassion when you see someone with not a rag to cover him, remembering how I was naked on the cross for you. If the nakedness of the poor man leaves you unmoved, remember mine'.

Compassion must not remain merely on the level of feeling but should be translated into action. Jesus was not only 'moved with compassion', but also 'went round doing good', 'curing every kind of disease and infirmity'. He loved and ministered to each individual sufferer. The Church's ministry to the sick is a continuation of Jesus' own healing ministry. The healing of bodies and souls was an intrinsic part of his work as Saviour.

There will always be individuals and groups in the Church who exemplify in a pre-eminent way this caring and healing ministry. The work begun by John of God is continued today by the Hospitallers who are everywhere renowned for their care of the mentally ill.

PETITION FOR THE PRAYER OF THE FAITHFUL

For all who minister to the mentally ill: that through their patience, compassion and professional skill, they may help these sufferers to lead full human lives.

9 March
SAINT FRANCES OF ROME, Religious

Memorial

REFLECTION

Born at Trastevere, Rome, in 1384, she was betrothed at the age of thirteen to the wealthy Lorenzo Ponziano. Although it was her desire to be a nun, she accepted her parents' decision with good grace. She was a good wife and mother, giving birth to three children, two of whom died at an early age. As well as managing the family household she found time to relieve the distress of Rome's poor, especially the sick poor. In the troubles of the time, her husband, who was a supporter of the legitimate pope, was singled out for attack by his enemies and lost his property. Frances stood by him and shared his trials. In 1425 she founded a society of devout women who were to live under the Rule of St Benedict while ministering to the poor. After her husband's death in 1436 she entered the community and became its first Superior and served in this capacity for the four remaining years of her life. She was canonised in 1648.

A very attractive trait of this saint is her gentleness. It was not of the soft kind. One could apply to her a dictum of St Francis de Sales: 'Nothing is as strong as gentleness, and nothing is as gentle as real strength'. It is said that never during their long years of married life was there a dispute between Frances and her husband. She was a peace-maker, winning over a very difficult daughter-in-law by patience and kindness. In the words of one of her companions (heard at the Office of Readings): 'God gave her such an abundance of loving-kindness that anyone who had dealings with her felt himself captivated by love and admiration for her.'

Love was the essence of her life, and this is affirmed in the Prayer of the day: 'Merciful Father, in Frances of Rome you have given us a unique example of love in marriage as well as in religious life'. There was a perfect continuity between her life as a wife and mother and that of a Benedictine Oblate and religious superior. Her total devotion to Christ and to the service of his poor gave unity to her life.

St Frances is an 'outstanding example of the married state and of the religious state'. Her life teaches us that these two states of life, rather than being opposed, are ways of the Christian life, the one complementing and supporting the other. It is not for us to decide which is superior, since this is a question of individual calling. Rather we should rejoice that married couples and consecrated religious share an identical call to be perfect. We need the witness and support of one another as we journey along our pilgrim way. The fidelity of married partners is a reminder to religious of their commitment to Christ and his kingdom. Religious, in their turn, can be a support to married people by the example of their lives. In whatever state of life we find ourselves, we should seek to discern God's presence and to follow him faithfully to the end of our days.

PETITION FOR THE PRAYER OF THE FAITHFUL

That we who are so easily vexed may learn from the gentleness and patience that characterised the life of St Frances of Rome.

10 March
SAINT JOHN OGILVIE, Priest and Martyr

Scotland: Feast

REFLECTION

Born at Drum-na-Leith, Scotland, John was brought up as a Calvinist. As a young boy he was sent to the Continent for his education. There he underwent a conversion and at the age of seventeen was received into the Catholic Church at the Scots College, Louvain. He entered the Society of Jesus, served in the French province, and was ordained at about the age of thirty.

With the fervour of a convert, ready to emulate the early martyrs, he volunteered for missionary work in his native Scotland. Posing as a horse dealer, and with the assumed name of John Watson, he entered that country where Catholic priests were proscribed. He had little success at first because of the intimidation of the Catholic populace. Disappointed, he set off for London to make contact with King James, and then went to Paris to report to his Superior General who rebuked him for leaving his post and ordered him to return to Scotland. After such delays and setbacks John Ogilvie began at least to find his feet and to make real headway.

He ministered to Catholic communities in Edinburgh and in Glasgow, instructed converts in the faith, baptised, and celebrated Mass. Impetuous by nature, he exposed himself to many risks. He was finally betrayed and arrested. His trial took place in Glasgow. There he was imprisoned and subjected to torture. He was condemned for high treason and sentenced to death by hanging in 1615. He was canonised by Pope Paul VI in 1976.

John Ogilvie was not a traitor. He recognised the temporal rights of the King. But in matters spiritual he owed allegiance to no one but Christ and to his vicar on earth. He died a martyr's death, for the faith and in defence of the freedom of human conscience.

'No greater love than this, that a man lay down his life for his friends'. St John Ogilvie died for love of Christ and his fellow men and women. We do no service to his memory by stirring up memories of ancient feuds. There is no place for bitterness now but only for sorrow that in an age of religious and political turmoil such terrible injustices could be perpetrated in the name of Christianity.

In his homily for the canonization of this Scottish martyr, Pope Paul VI strikes an irenical and ecumenical note. Acknowledging the saint's contribution to the cause of religious freedom, he concludes: 'On this account the saint, venerated by us, far from being a symbol of religious difference, will soften the unhappy memory of violence or of the abuse of authority in the interest of religion, and will help us to resolve the divisions relating to our respective creeds into sentiments of mutual respect, of calm research into and faithful adherence to the Truth in order to recover that longed-for unity of faith and love which Christ taught us was the supreme expression of his gospel.'

PETITION FOR THE PRAYER OF THE FAITHFUL

That the Catholic Church in Scotland, now suffering a decline in priestly and religious vocations, may derive inspiration and strength from the example of St John Ogilvie and of the many men and women who assisted him in his mission.

17 March
SAINT PATRICK, Bishop, Patron of Ireland

Ireland: Solemnity
United Kingdom and Australia: Feast

REFLECTION

It is not easy to discern the real St Patrick behind the legends. It is fortunate that we possess in his *Confessio* not only reliable information about his life but also an authentic self-portrait.

Born in Britain about 390, of Christian parents, the young Patrick was captured by Irish pirates and sold as a slave. For six years he toiled as a herdsmen. In the hardship and loneliness of his life he underwent a profound conversion and gave himself wholeheartedly to prayer. Having found a means of escape he returned to his home in Britain. But there in a dream he heard the Irish people calling him back. He was to return not as a slave but as an apostle. And so he trained for the priesthood and was in time consecrated a bishop. On his return to Ireland about 435 he worked principally in the northern part of the country. With utter trust in God he laboured indefatigably amid difficulties and dangers. By the time of his death about 461, the Church was firmly established in Ireland.

How different is the Patrick of the *Confessio* from the blown-up caricature! In his own eyes he was no super-man. He was all too aware of his own limitations, his lack of education and his unworthiness. He regarded himself simply as an instrument chosen by God to bring about the conversion of the pagan Irish. The achievements of his ministry were all to be attributed to the 'gift of God'. He expresses this in a strong and homely image: 'I was a stone lying in a deep mire, and he that is mighty came and in his mercy lifted me up and placed me on top of the wall'.

Patrick continues to speak to the Irish people. The *Confessio* is addressed to this people from whom he received much ill treatment but for whom he was prepared to lay down his life: 'Should I be worthy, I am ready to give even my life, promptly and gladly, for his name; And it is there [in Ireland] that I wish to spend it until I die, if the Lord should graciously allow me'.

It was Patrick's prayer that the Irish people would never fall away from the faith: 'Wherefore may it never happen to me from my God that I should ever lose the people which he has purchased from the ends of the earth'. In the light of scandals and of rapid cultural and social change, the Church in his country may be facing its greatest challenge. As Pope John Paul II declared on his visit here in 1979: 'Ireland must choose; you the present generation of Irish people must decide; your choice must be clear and your decision firm'. Our prayer today is that not only will we 'keep the faith' but that we may also continue to 'proclaim to the world the good news of salvation'.

PETITIONS FOR THE PRAYER OF THE FAITHFUL

That the land where Patrick preached the Gospel of peace may be a place where Christians of all traditions may live together in mutual respect and tolerance.

That Irish men and women who serve as missionaries in foreign lands may experience the support of our prayers and know that their work is highly valued by the Church.

That Ireland at this critical juncture of its history may remain true to the faith preached by Patrick, whose prayer was that 'the people purchased from the ends of the earth might never be lost'.

18 March
SAINT CYRIL OF JERUSALEM
Bishop and Doctor of the Church

Memorial

REFLECTION

St Cyril was Bishop of Jerusalem from 348 to 386. Embroiled in the Arian controversies of the time, his episcopacy was a stormy one. His most bitter opponent was a fellow-bishop of Arian tendencies, one Acacius, who used intrigue to have him twice banished form his see. Such unjust treatment would have embittered a lesser man, but throughout the ordeal Cyril maintained his peace-loving and gentle disposition. The last eight years of his life were spent in secure possession of his see, but there were also troubled by bitter factions in Jerusalem and by the prevailing low moral standards. Cyril was present at the Council of Constantinople in 981 which promulgated the Nicene Creed in an emended form.

This fourth-century bishop is best remembered for his *Catecheses*, a collection of eighteen pre-baptismal catechetical lectures. These provide a comprehensive and wholly orthodox presentation of the main doctrines of the Catholic faith for those shortly to be baptised. They are of considerable doctrinal importance and serve as an inspiration to all who are engaged in the catechumenal movement of our own time. We can read an extract of one of these instructions in the second lesson of the Office of Readings.

In his long ministry of preaching Cyril consistently defended the doctrine of the divinity of Christ against the insinuations of the Arians. For this he endured persecution and exile. The Church reveres him as one who led the Christian people to 'a deeper understanding of the mysteries of baptism and the Eucharist'. And, since he expounded so well the doctrine of the true nature of Christ, we ask that he may now help us to grow in knowledge of God's Son so that 'we may have life and have it more abundantly'.

PETITION FOR THE PRAYER OF THE FAITHFUL

For all who instruct others in the faith – parents, teachers, catechists – that their lives and actions may confirm the truth of their words.

19 March
SAINT JOSEPH
Husband of the Blessed Virgin Mary

Solemnity

REFLECTION

The little we know about Joseph's life is derived from Matthew's and Luke's Gospels. He was of Davidic descent but poor, a carpenter by trade. Apocryphal writings supplement this with legendary accounts and make him out to be an old man. Eastern Christianity was ahead of the West in venerating him in personal devotion and in public worship. In the Western Church we find his name first inscribed in the eighth century Martyrologies. His feast was celebrated in England before the year 1100. In later centuries his popularity owes much to saints such as Bernardine of Siena and Teresa of Avila. In 1870 he was declared Patron of the Universal Church by Pope Pius IX.

'Though he is dead, he still speaks by faith'. So declares the Letter to the Hebrews in the extract for the Office of Readings (11:1-16). The readings of the Office and Mass also highlight the faith of Joseph. His was a robust, practical kind of faith. Like Abraham he 'hoped and believed' (Rom 4:8). Deservedly is he placed among the great men and women of the Old Testament. Once he understood what God wanted of him he act promptly: 'He did what the angel of the Lord told him to do' (Mt 1:24). In him faith and obedience went hand in hand: 'Faith and deeds worked together; his faith became perfect by what he did' (Responsory). His was indeed 'the obedience of faith.'

Man of faith, he was also a provider and protector. Like the Patriarch Joseph he was entrusted with something precious. 'God made him father of the King and Lord of all his household' (Gen 45:8; responsory for second reading). St Bernardine of Siena declares: 'He was chosen by the eternal Father to be the faithful foster-parent and guardian of the most precious treasures of God, his Son and his spouse'. The intercession for Evening Prayer and the concluding prayer draw inspiration from this theme: 'Joseph took the child Jesus into his care, loving and accepting him as his own son. May we accept all that God gives us, and care for those entrusted to us'. 'May his prayer still help your Church to be an equally faithful guardian of your mysteries'.

PETITIONS FOR THE PRAYER OF THE FAITHFUL

For parents: that the example of their lives and the witness of their faith may lead their children to know and love Christ.

For priests, deacons and all ministers of the Gospel. May they hear and heed the words of Paul to Timothy: 'You have been trusted to look after something precious; guard it with the help of the Holy Spirit who lives in us' (2 Tim 1:14).

For all of us: that through the prayers of Joseph we may be led to a life of closer union with Christ, the Incarnate Word.

23 March
SAINT TURIBIUS OF MONGROVEJO, Bishop
Memorial

REFLECTION

This Spanish-born missionary prelate is one of the great saints of South America. A lawyer by profession, he was prevailed upon to receive orders and was made Archbishop of Lima, Peru, which was then a Spanish colony. He arrived there in 1581 and was faced with an immense task. His diocese included four hundred miles of coastline. Much of the land was mountainous and covered with forest. In addition, there were serious abuses among the clergy, widespread ignorance of Christian teaching among the people, and shameful exploitation of the poor Indians by the Spanish conquerors.

Turibius set to work right away, holding councils, founding seminaries, disciplining refractory clergy. But what we admire most is not his reforming zeal but his championing of the poor. He attacked the worst excesses of colonialism, and with some effect. He thereby incurred the enmity of those in power and of corrupt officials. It may be noted that his option for the poor included impoverished Spaniards as well as native Indians.

This prelate did not remain in his palace and write pastorals. He went out on visitation. It took him seven years to cover his vast diocese, parts of which were almost inaccessible. There were few roads and no means of transport other than by mule or on foot. Turibius wished to speak directly to the people and not by means of an intermediary. To this end he learnt a number of Indian dialects and continued learning new dialects right up to his death in 1606.

The pastoral office of a bishop has been well described in one of the Decrees of the Second Vatican Council. An extract is given for the Office of Readings and is aptly chosen for today's commemoration: 'In exercising their office of father and pastor, the bishops should be among their own people as those who serve, good shepherds who know their own sheep and whose sheep know them; true fathers, outstanding in the spirit of love and carefulness towards all'.

The claim that St Turibius was 'one of the greatest missionary prelates of the New World' is a valid one. His struggle to redress injustice and exploitation continues to inspire bishops and priests in Latin America who not only preach good news to the poor but are also their champions in the cause of human rights and better living standards.

The prayer of the feast speaks of his 'pastoral care and zeal for truth'. It acknowledges his role in building up the Church in Peru. His *cultus* is no longer confined to that country but has been extended to the universal Church since the inclusion of this saint in the Roman Calendar of 1969. He deserves to be known and venerated as much as his two great contemporaries – St Rose of Lima and St Martin de Porres.

PETITION FOR THE PRAYER OF THE FAITHFUL

For all pastors in Latin America who are committed to evangelization and the championing of the poor. May they be given strength and endurance.

25 March
THE ANNUNCIATION OF THE LORD

Solemnity

REFLECTION

This solemnity has been celebrated in the Western Church since the seventh century, in the East since the sixth century. The reformed Calendar of 1969 restored its original title of *Adnuntiatio Domini*, making it clear that this is primarily a feast of Christ. For centuries it had been known as the Annunciation of the Blessed Virgin Mary. What is foremost in today's celebration is the mystery of the Incarnation. According to patristic tradition, it was at the moment of the Annunciation, when Mary uttered her consent, that the eternal Word was conceived. We recall this in the prayer of the *Angelus* at the words: 'The Angel of the Lord declared unto Mary, and she conceived of the Holy Spirit'.

While primarily a feast of Christ, the Annunciation is also a feast of Mary. That is because the lives and destinies of Mother and Son are inseparably interwoven. As Pope Paul VI declared in his encyclical *Marialis Cultus*: 'the feast was and is a joint one of Christ and the Blessed Virgin: of the Word who becomes Son of Mary and of the Virgin who becomes Mother of God'. Situated between the two great poles of the Church's year, Christmas and Easter, the Annunciation recalls the mystery of the Incarnation and at the same time anticipates the obedience unto death of Holy Week. Incarnation and Redemption, let us now consider these two mysteries in the light of today's celebration.

The incarnational aspect is evoked in the third antiphon at Vespers: 'The Word humbled himself today for us and became man'. This introduces the canticle from Philippians 2:6-11 which recalls how Christ Jesus 'emptied himself to assume the condition of a slave and became as men are'. It was at the consent of Mary, the lowly handmaid, and by the power of the Holy Spirit that the divine Word came to dwell among us (Intercessions).

In the Office of Readings we are addressed by Pope St Leo the Great, the great Doctor of the Incarnation. The reading is taken from his famous 'Tome'. His teaching is summed up in the concluding words:

> For it must be said that one and the same Jesus is truly Son of God and truly Son of man. He is God insofar as in the beginning he was the Word, and the Word was with God. And he is man insofar as the Word became flesh and dwelt among us.

The concluding prayer is inspired by this profound doctrine: 'Shape us in the likeness of the divine nature of our Redeemer, whom we believe to be true God and true man, since it is by your will, Lord God, the he your Word should take to himself our human nature in the womb of the Blessed Virgin' (Breviary version).

And now we turn to the redemptive aspect. It is interesting to learn of an ancient tradition according to which Jesus was crucified on the anniversary of his conception. It is also significant that in the Byzantine rite this feast is commemorated even if it falls within the Easter Triduum. This is sound theology since the incarnation is the 'beginning of the redemption', to use an expression of Pope Paul VI. It is the first act of Christ's priestly ministry.

It is appropriate that the Letter to the Hebrews should form part of this day's liturgy. In the Second Reading at Mass (Heb 10:4-10) Christ, speaking through the inspired author, declares: 'You wanted no sacrifice or oblation ... then I said, "God, here I am, I am coming to obey your will".' 'Behold I come' – '*Ecce venio*' – this announces the theme of the Eucharistic Liturgy. It is proclaimed in the entrance song and taken up again in the responsorial psalm. And not forgetting the dual character of this feast, it is good for us today to set side by side Mary's act of obedience with that of her incarnate Son. The *Fiat* ('Be it done unto me') of Mary and the *Ecce venio* of Christ so coincide as to become almost a single act of obedience.

Blessed Columba Marmion, reflecting on this mystery, declares in *Christ the Life of the Soul:*

> This *fiat* is Mary's consent to the divine plan of redemption; this *fiat* is like the echo of the *fiat* of creation. But it is a new world, an infinitely higher world, a world of grace that God himself creates after this consent; for at this moment the Divine Word, the second Person of the Holy Trinity, becomes incarnate in Mary: *Et Verbum caro factum est.*

PETITIONS FOR THE PRAYER OF THE FAITHFUL

May our hearts be open, as was Mary's, to receive God's Word and to be generous in responding to it.

May Christ become a living presence in the lives of those who are empty and unfulfilled.

May we accept the joys and sufferings of life in a spirit of obedient faith, ready to do God's will at all times.

April

2 April
SAINT FRANCIS OF PAOLA, Hermit

Memorial

REFLECTION

This Francis was a native of Paola, a seaside town of Calabria in the most southern region of Italy. While still an adolescent he chose to live as a hermit in a cave overlooking the sea. This early association with the sea, together with later miracles connected with the sea, explains why in our own time he has been declared patron saint of seafarers.

Sanctity has a magnetic quality. This solitary was joined by companions wishing to emulate his austere life and to live under his direction. Thus was born a new religious order in the

Church. Here was a band of men intent on living the evangelical ideal of renunciation to its extreme limit. But they were bonded together by mutual love. *Caritas* (love) was their motto, and the expression 'out of love' was constantly on the lips of Francis. Austerity not tempered by love repels rather than attracts. The saint's genuine humanity and kindness drew people to him and made him everywhere popular.

Humility was the hallmark of this new order. To distinguish his followers from other Franciscans, St Francis called them the 'Minim Friars'. There were not 'Friars Minor', but *Minimi* – the least of the friars. The title was not really so inappropriate since the first recruits were poor, uneducated men, and Francis himself had received little formal education.

In time his fame spread well beyond Italy. He was summoned to France to assist the dying King Louis XI and he remained for many years in that country acting as counsellor and at times envoy to the monarchy. But this in no way affected his deep-rooted humility. His mission in France was undertaken under obedience to the Holy See.

It is this exemplary humility that is brought to our attention in the prayer proper to this day. It goes : 'Father of the lowly (*Deus humilium celsitudo*), you raised St Francis of Paola to the glory of the saints; by his example and prayers may we come to the rewards you have promised the humble'. The prayer echoes Mary's *Magnificat* and the Sermon on the Mount. Humility becomes those who seek to follow Christ who himself chose this path of lowliness. It is a fundamental law of the Christian life that 'God opposes the proud but accords his grace to the humble' (1 Pet 5:5).

A lover of peace and harmony, Francis of Paola strove to maintain a spirit of mutual tolerance and fraternal love among the Brothers. A letter of his, read at today's Office, should be of importance to every family and community. It is an impassioned appeal to put aside differences and to forget old injuries. It concludes : 'Be lovers of peace, the most precious treasure that anyone can desire ... Live in such a way that you will bring upon yourselves the blessing of God, and that the peace of God the Father will be with you always'.

A final note. The penances and mortifications of the saints are not greatly to our liking today. And yet the message of the cross and the call to self-conquest have relevance for every age. The rigorous discipline that Francis of Paola chose for himself and the friars seems to have won divine approval by the fact that he died on Good Friday in 1507 at the very hour of the Lord's sacred passion. He was then ninety-one!

PETITION FOR THE PRAYER OF THE FAITHFUL

For all the followers of St Francis of Paola who courageously pursue the evangelical idea of poverty and who gladly serve Christ in the least of his brethren.

4 April

SAINT ISIDORE, Bishop and Doctor of the Church

Memorial

REFLECTION

Even the Dark Ages had its luminaries, and St Isidore (560-636) was one of the greatest of these. He has been well described as 'the schoolmaster of the Middle Ages'. His learning was prodigious, and his writings ranged from theological works to treatises on natural science. But he was no mere academician. As Bishop of Seville for thirty-seven years, he worked tirelessly to convert the followers of Arianism, to further Church reform and to make education available to greater numbers of young people. He was an enlightened and liberal educationalist.

St Isidore represents the best kind of Christian humanist, one who combines the love of learning with the desire for God. For him, study and prayer went hand in hand, and his reading of Scripture and the Fathers was of the sapiential and prayerful kind which monks describe by the term *lectio divina* (divine or sacred reading).

On this subject let us hear him in his own words in an extract from his *Book of Sentences* selected for the Office of Readings. Here he shows the need to combine reading with meditation and prayer. He says:

> If anyone wants to be always with God, he ought to pray often and read often as well. For when we pray, it is we who talk to God, whereas when we read, it is God who speaks to us.

He is aware that the grace of God must touch the heart, the Holy Spirit must speak to us if we are to understand the Scriptures: 'The Word of God, heard with the ears, only then reaches the depths of the heart, when the grace of God touches the mind within, so that it can understand'.

As the prayer for his feast-day declares, St Isidore enriched the Church with his teaching. His books were widely read and very influential in the Middle Ages and later. Though little read today, they form part of the rich patrimony of the Church.

Isidore of Seville is included among the great ecclesiastical teachers on whom the title Doctor of the Church is conferred. Of them it can be truly said: 'The learned will shine as brightly as the vault of heaven, and those who have instructed many in virtue will shine like the stars for all eternity' (antiphon for Morning Prayer). And since we always have need of the wisdom of the saints, it is appropriate that we should address this great teacher and pastor in these words: 'O holy doctor, Saint Isidore, light of the Church; lover of the Law of God, pray for us to the Son of God' (antiphon for the *Magnificat*).

PETITION FOR THE PRAYER OF THE FAITHFUL

For teachers and theologians: that the gift of wisdom may be theirs, along with the readiness to place their knowledge at the service of the Church.

5 April
SAINT VINCENT FERRER, Priest

Memorial

REFLECTION

Born at Valencia in 1350, son of an Englishman, Vincent joined the Dominicans at the age of seventeen. Brilliant in his studies, he quickly won distinction as a philosopher and preacher. He preached with extraordinary effect in extended tours through Spain, France, Switzerland and Italy, calling on the men and women of his time to renounce sin and to turn to God. His was a stern message: sin, judgement, repentance, were recurring themes. He spoke hard, uncompromising words, but he did so with compassion. The impact he made on people seems to have stemmed from his personal sanctity and the burning sincerity with which he spoke.

Apart from his preaching, Vincent Ferrer will always be remembered for the part he played in bringing about an end to the Great Western Schism (1378–1414) – a sad episode in the Church's history when there were two, and later even three, claimants to the papal throne. The saint undermined his own health in trying to persuade the stubborn Peter de Luna, the pope at Avignon, to renounce his claim. But in the end the long, patient negotiations of Vincent Ferrer bore fruit and the schism was healed.

He was happiest when preaching, which he often did in the open air to accommodate the large crowds. The last three years of his life were spent in Normandy and Brittany, preaching constantly and effecting many conversions. He died at Vannes, Brittany, on this day in 1419 in his seventieth year.

What, we may ask, was the secret of Vincent's success as a preacher? And what is it that makes a good preacher? Part of the answer is given by the saint himself in the passage read today in the Office of Readings. There he advises the preacher to use simple language, adopt a conversational style and to give plenty of examples. Most important of all, he must speak with love. Even when refuting error, denouncing vice, calling to obedience, he will 'speak out of the depths of love and fatherly care'. Only in this way will his words bear fruit. In a later age the truth of this would be expressed in a characteristic saying of St Francis de Sales : 'He who speaks with love speaks effectively'.

A popular preacher who did not preach popular themes: that was his vocation as a Friar Preacher and as a man sent by God. The prayer of the feast alludes to this : 'Father, you called Saint Vincent Ferrer to preach the gospel of the last Judgement...' Jesus began his preaching with the summons, 'Repent and believe the good news'. The call to repentance, conversion of heart – these are vital to the ministry of preaching, and so are valid for every age including our own.

PETITION FOR THE PRAYER OF THE FAITHFUL

For all who exercise a ministry of the word in the Church: preaching Christ crucified, may they draw men and women to Christ by the sincerity of their words and the uprightness of the lives.

7 April
SAINT JOHN BAPTIST DE LA SALLE, Priest

Memorial

REFLECTION

The founder of the Brothers of the Christian Schools was born at Rheims, France, in 1651. He entered the seminary of St Sulpice in 1678. On the death of his parents he inherited a large fortune. With his wealth and influence he seemed destined for high ecclesiastical office. But God was calling him to renounce all such advantages and to devote his life to the education of the poor. He gave away all his wealth, directing it to the relief of the poor and famine-stricken. He set up a number of schools for poor boys and recruited a number of dedicated lay teachers. From among these men there was formed the nucleus of what was to become the Brothers of the Christian Schools. These he trained in his own ideals and methods. Courageous and innovative, he revolutionised the teaching methods of his time.

It is interesting to learn that at the request of King James I of England he set up a school for the sons of Irish emigrants in France. It is also noteworthy that he established in France the first training college for teachers.

With so many achievements it could be thought that his life was easy. It was not. He had to endure much opposition inside his order as well as from outside. He bore many crosses, and it was appropriate that he should be declared the patron of all school-teachers.

The second reading from the Divine Office is taken from a *Meditation* of the saint. It witnesses to the love that inspired his work and drove him on, the love which was to motivate all Brothers of the Christian Schools. Theirs was to be a service of love, they were to give without counting the cost.

The prayer of the day acknowledges that God raised up John Baptist de la Salle for the vital task of educating the young in the Christian faith, a challenging task which in our day fewer and fewer seem prepared to take on. The vocation of the teaching Brother is not an easy or congenial one. But God, who raised up John Baptist de la Salle to provide education for those for whom no provision was made, continues to call generous young men and women to work for the disadvantaged, to provide for them an education that is human and Christian.

PETITION FOR THE PRAYER OF THE FAITHFUL

For all teachers and especially for the Brothers of the Christian Schools. In all their difficulties may they have unshaken confidence in the grace of Jesus Christ.

11 April
SAINT STANISLAUS, Bishop and Martyr

Memorial

REFLECTION

St Stanislaus epitomises the indomitable spirit of Polish Catholicism. In 1030 he became Bishop of Krakow and soon won renown as a reformer, a zealous preacher and a great lover of the poor. He openly opposed the king, Boleslav II, for his tyrannical and immoral ways. For this courageous stand he was murdered while celebrating Mass on this day in 1079.

Today we invoke this bishop-martyr to assist the people of Poland that they may continue to exhibit that robust and tenacious faith that has been an inspiration to the whole Christian world. And when our own faith is put to the test we remember the words of Scripture: 'Happy the man who stands firm when struggles come. He has proved himself, and will win the prize of life, the crown that the Lord has promised to those who love him' (Jam 1:12).

Nine hundred years after his death a Pole came to occupy the papal throne. John Paul II had obviously been inspired by this patron of his country: one indication of this is the fact that he raised this feast to the rank of obligatory memorial in 1979.

History repeats itself. Just a hundred years later than Stanislaus, another sacrilegious murder would be perpetrated against a bishop – the murder of the Archbishop of Canterbury, Thomas Becket, in his cathedral on December 29, 1179.

The similar circumstances of their martyrdoms suggests a final reflection which has to do with the intimate connection between the Eucharist and martyrdom. 'Imitate what you are carrying out' – *Imitamini quod tractatis* – is the exhortation the priest receives at his ordination. This echoes a theme that is characteristic of the writings of the Fathers. It was especially dear to St Cyprian, the third-century bishop, who lived so close to the martyrs of North Africa and himself met a martyr's death. It is

Cyprian who addresses us in the second reading of the Office and shows how the martyr draws strength from the Eucharist: 'Let us also arm our right hand with the sword of the Spirit, so that this right hand which receives the body of the Lord, may, mindful of the Eucharist, embrace him, and afterwards may receive the prize of the heavenly crown from the Lord.'

PETITION FOR THE PRAYER OF THE FAITHFUL

For the people of Poland: that they may live in freedom and remain steadfast in the profession of their Christian and Catholic faith.

13 April
SAINT MARTIN, Pope and Martyr

Memorial

REFLECTION

St Martin was the last of the popes to be martyred, not by execution but by a long-drawn-out agony of imprisonment and exile. Born at Todi in Umbria, he became Pope in 649 A.D. In his defence of the orthodox faith and assertion of the Church rights he incurred the wrath of Emperor Constans II who had him banished to Kherson in the Crimea. There began his Calvary which ended on this day in 656.

As well as the being the last pope-martyr, St Martin has the distinction of being honoured by the Churches of both East and West. His feast-day is included in the Byzantine Calendar, celebrated also on this day. Because he opposed the heresy which claimed that Christ had a divine but not a human will (monothelitism), he is revered as 'the glorious defender of the Orthodox faith'.

In the Greek *Life of St Martin* we are told that he was 'a noble model for all who want to live piously and suffer for the real truth. Indeed he bore his trials nobly and never compromised on matters of principle. From one of his letters from exile, selected for the Office of Readings, we get some idea of his sufferings. It is poignant without being self-pitying, reproachful of his false friends and yet forgiving, urging the Christians of Rome to remain steadfast in the truth and to be loyal to his successor on the papal throne.

A pope from the distant past, caught up in the politics and doctrinal conflicts of his time, it is not easy for us to relate to him today. And yet, as the prayer of the day reminds us, we too need 'the grace to bear the hardships of this life'. Bearing our own cross, we can still be encouraged by him 'whom no threats could daunt, no pains and penalties break'.

Martin triumphed by steadfastness and love. At the end of his days he could exclaim with St Paul: 'I have fought the good fight to the end; I have run the race to the finish; I have kept the faith' (2 Tim 4:7).

On the feast of Pope St Martin I we would do well to pray for his successor. Each holder of the papal office must endure a kind of martyrdom, bearing the burden of all the Churches and the responsibility for the orthodoxy of faith. Like the first pope, himself imprisoned and martyred, he is a 'St Peter in chains'.

PETITION FOR THE PRAYER OF THE FAITHFUL

For the Pope and all pastors of the Church: that they may be wise and courageous leaders of the flock of Christ.

The Dominican Publications website
– www.DominicanPublications.com –
keeps you informed
about our books on
religious life
liturgy
preaching aids
spirituality
current problems

and about our magazines
doctrine & life
RELIGIOUS LIFE REVIEW
Scripture in Church
Spirituality

www.DominicanPublications.com

Also by Flor McCarthy

New Sunday and Holy Day Liturgies
Year A,
Year B
Year C

- three homilies for each occasion
- additional stories
- Scripture notes
- introductions, headings, and prayers of the faithful

Three volumes, each 376 pp., sewn paperbacks
Each volume €19.99

The Gospel of the Heart
Offers encouragement, hope and fresh insights to everyone who seeks to put new vigour into understanding the Christian message, and into living its Gospel.
176 pp. Pbk €11.99

Liturgies for Weddings
Will be of great help to celebrants. Also a book which a couple might buy – or which a priest might give as a gift – as a boost to their confidence and idealism.
144 pp. Pbk €11.99

Funeral Liturgies
Thirty-eight full liturgies plus 29 Reflections, 10 Prayer Services, and 4 rites of committal – all stressing the power of the word of God to offer hope amidst sadness.
272 pp. Pbk €12.99

*In all cases, post and packing extra: 20% (Ireland & Britain)
Other countries: please apply for rates – fax or email*

Dominican Publications 42 PARNELL SQUARE, DUBLIN 1
Fax +353-(0)1-873-1760   *Email* Sales@DominicanPublications.com

North American orders to COSTELLO PUBLISHING COMPANY, INC.
Box 9. Northport, Long Island, NY 11768, USA